THE PEOPLES OF INDIA

First published 1913
This edition published by Lector House in 2024

ISBN: 978-93-6138-008-2

Lector House LLP
Registered Office: H. No. 96, Block C, Tomar Colony,
Burari, Delhi – 110084, India
info@lectorhouse.com
www.lectorhouse.com

THE PEOPLES OF INDIA

JAMES DRUMMOND ANDERSON

2024

LECTOR HOUSE LLP

Brāhmans
(Mirzapur district)

THE PEOPLES OF INDIA

BY

J. D. ANDERSON, M.A.

Teacher of Bengali in the University of Cambridge,
formerly of the Indian Civil Service

Preface

THE writing of this little book has been delayed by the hope I once cherished of incorporating in it some of the results of the Indian Census of 1911. This desire was inevitable in the case of a retired Indian official, who, like most of his kind, has taken a small part in one or more of the decennial numberings of the Indian people. In this country, a Census affords material chiefly for the calculations and theories of the statistician, and the Registrar-General is not regarded as an expert in Anthropology or Linguistics. But in India the case is very different. If the district officer is always glad to learn as much as possible of the people with whom he is brought into contact, his official duties often reveal only the seamy side of Indian life, and it is only when he is in camp, or snatching a rare and hurried holiday in shooting, that he gets to see something of the people otherwise than as litigants or payers of revenue. A census is an agreeable and welcome opportunity for looking at India from another and more genially human point of view. In the first place, it is one of the least expensive of official operations, since it is chiefly performed by unpaid and volunteer agency. Hence the official, a little weary of litigants, touts, pleaders, and subordinates, who, however amiable in their private lives, are apt to be indolent and obstructive in office, is glad to make acquaintance with new friends, who, for the most part, take an intelligent and amused interest in the unfamiliar task of numbering. For many busy weeks before the actual counting takes place, the district officer has to ride far and near, to satisfy himself that all necessary preparations have duly been made, to issue the instructions that may be called for by the zeal, inquisitiveness or density of his volunteer colleagues. In the process, he has many pleasant and some amusing experiences. On one occasion I rode into a little village on the north-eastern frontier, inhabited by semi-savage Tibeto-Burmese people. Official orders as to the numbering of all the house in legible figures had apparently not been obeyed. I simulated wrath and disappointment, but the worthy headman on whom I vented my (purely official) indignation was not dismayed. "Bring out your drums!" he shouted. Every householder produced the family kettle-drum, on the head of which the number of his house had been duly inscribed in large figures. There was no paper in the village, but parchment was invented before paper, and the headman deserved the commendation I was glad to bestow. On another occasion, I found a house numbered indeed, but grievously dilapidated and obviously deserted. "Why is this empty house numbered?" I asked. "It is haunted by a ghost, sir," answered the enumerator. I confess I felt sorry not to allow him to include this ghostly visitant in a census of living men. Other incidents, more ethnologically important than these, will frequently occur. In any case the Census Report of an Indian province is by far the most interesting official document in existence, and each census adds something to our knowledge of Indian humanity, if only because each Census Commissioner, always an officer of unusual ability and attainments, looks at his task from a point of view somewhat different from that of his predecessors, and stamps his individuality on the work of his subordinates. Those who have read Mr E. A. Gait's article on *Caste* in the *Dictionary of Ethics and Religion* will expect the census of 1911 to contain new views and fresh information as to the actual working of the caste system in various provinces, and its relation to the religious ideas of the people.

It was natural, then, that I should wish to learn from a new tapping of the source from which has been compiled, for the most part, the ethnical portion of the first volume of the Imperial Gazetteer of India, which has been my chief authority in compiling this little book. But I know not when Mr Gait's Report for all India will be ready, and even the Provincial Reports come but slowly from the Press. Most of them are full of the most interesting and valuable information, but it takes time to assimilate so much new matter, and, in any case, not much of it could have been utilized for so small and elementary a book. Hence I have simply to state my debt to the late Sir H. H. Risley and Mr E. A. Gait for the chapter on Race and Caste; to Sir G. A. Grierson for the chapter on Languages, and to Mr William Crooke for enabling me further to summarise his masterly summary of what is known about Indian Religions. It is a particular pleasure to acknowledge my indebtedness to my friend Sir G. A. Grierson. Years ago, when we were young men, it was known that in him the Indian Civil Service possessed a scholar and a linguist of most unusual industry and ability. But few knew that there was germinating in his mind the scheme for the great *Linguistic Survey of India*, the most remarkable feat of administrative scholarship, perhaps, that has ever been attempted, a feat that has won him the *Prix Volney* and I know not what other appreciations of his work in France and Germany. His learning and linguistic skill are widely known, but I must seize the opportunity to tell of another feature of his achievement. Of course no man knows more than a few of the hundreds of Indian languages, but there is one man who knows something of the working and mechanism of them all, and that is Sir G. A. Grierson. I had the privilege of helping him with part of the Bodo volume of his *Survey*, having had occasion to learn one or two Tibeto-Burman languages in the course of official duty. The practised ease with which he acquired the syntactical and phonetic peculiarities of languages with which he had no previous acquaintance was the most surprising and delightful intellectual performance I have ever witnessed.

I have ventured occasionally to enliven my chiefly borrowed narrative with personal ideas or reminiscences. Such digressions have however been few and brief, and I do not think I need apologise for them.

I have to thank Miss Lilian Whitehouse and my son, Lieut. M. A. Anderson, R.E., for the two diagrammatic maps which will, I hope, clear up any geographical difficulties created by a necessarily brief account of a large and complicated subject.

I owe the illustrations of caste types to the kindness of Mr William Crooke. They are from photographs of inhabitants of one single district of the United Provinces and are interesting as showing how in a single small area racial differences show themselves in such a way as to be recognisable by the most careless observer. They prove once more how stratified Indian humanity has become under the influence of caste rules of marriages.

J. D. A.

September, 1913.

Contents

List of Plates

List of Maps

Page

Introduction

It is necessary, once more, to remind the reader that the peninsula of India has an area and population roughly equal to the area and population of Europe without Russia. Everyone who has learnt geography at school is familiar with the great triangle, its base in the soaring Himalayan heights in the north, its apex jutting into the Indian Ocean, and marked by the satellite island of Ceylon. To the north, then, is the great mountain barrier, a tangled mass of snowy peaks, glaciers and snowfields, separating the sunny plains of India proper from the plateaux of Central Asia. Beneath them lie wide river basins, sandy and dry as unirrigated Egypt to the west; moist, warm, and waterlogged to the east. To the south of the valleys of the Indus and the Ganges is the central plateau, home of many aboriginal races. This rises on the west into a castellated rampart of hills facing the Arabian Sea, and on the south slopes away into green undulating uplands. So much, at least, of geographical description must be given as a clue to the distribution of the peoples of India. Along the Himalayas, growing stronger in numbers as we go eastwards, are races mostly of a Mongolian type, mingled with purely Indian elements. In the Panjāb and the United Provinces, sending offshoots southwards along the well-watered west coast, are the peoples in whom the traces of Aryan immigration are most visible. In Bengal we find a duskier race, provisionally termed Mongolo-Dravidian, but with a strong infusion, in the upper classes, of western blood. In the south are a still darker population almost wholly Dravidian. It is in the most ancient part of India, in the high plateau of the Deccan, that there still dwell the peoples who are probably the aborigines of the land and use the most purely Indian languages, the various Dravidian dialects. The geologically recent valleys of the Indus and Ganges are the home of races, mingled with aboriginal peoples, whose language and physical features show that in them is a strong strain of immigrant blood.

On the Himalayan slopes, in Assam, and especially in Burma, are Tibeto-Burman peoples, with something of a Japanese aspect. Intermingled with all these, in forests and on rough and hardly accessible hills, are scattered many groups of semi-savage folk, of whom little was known till the gradual spread of British rule carried the administrator, the missionary, and finally the anthropologist, into regions once considered unfit for the presence of civilised men.

So far, it may be said, the distribution of Indian humanity is not very unlike that of the races of Europe. Even this very crude summary, it is true, shows at least three great groups of languages, Dravidian in the south, Indo-European in the west and north-west, Tibeto-Burman in the north and the north-east. There are in fact five separate families of human speech which have their homes in India; the Aryan, the Dravidian, the Mundā, the Mon-Khmer, and the Tibeto-Chinese. The lateral spread of these is, of course, no real indication of the present habitat of five different races of men. But they do indicate the existence, in varying degrees of purity, of five different origins, of which the Dravidian and Mundā alone can be said to be purely indigenous and confined to the Indian peninsula. Nowhere is it more easy than in India to see how languages spread from race to race, from tribe to tribe, with a sort of linguistic contagion; the stronger, more supple, more copious, more cultivated languages replacing and gradually destroying weaker forms of speech. Something of the same sort has occurred, and is even now happening, in Europe. But the surviving European languages are mostly sturdy and vigorous, and do not readily yield place to one another. In India the process of linguistic invasion is going on before our eyes, attendant on the gradual growth of Hindu civilisation and religion, which disdains to practise open and reasoned proselytism, but extends its borders nevertheless, and carries with it one or another of the Aryan dialects.

In spite of the spread of the stronger languages, the five great families of Indian speech remain and testify to more varied origins than those of

Europe. One of the first results of familiarity with Indian peoples is a sense of their remarkable variety of aspect and culture. When the stranger lands in India, his first feeling is one of bewildering sameness; the dusky beings that surround him seem as like one another as sheep, or peas. But that sensation is merely due to the predominance of unfamiliar colour, and soon gives way to an impression of astonishing and most interesting variety. This variety is exhibited by the careful anthropometric investigations of the ethnologist. But there is more variety than average measurements show, and the rough impressions of the experienced administrator and traveller are not without their value. For instance, Sir William Hunter, in his work on *The Indian Empire*, classified the highlanders of Chota Nagpore as a race apart, whom he called Kolārians. Sir H. H. Risley says that "the distinction between Kolārians and Dravidians is purely linguistic, and does not correspond to any differences of physical type." As a matter of average physical measurements, this criticism is just. The average dimensions of Sonthal skulls are the same as those of other Dravidian races. But he would be a poor observer of racial characteristics, who could not pick out a typical inhabitant of Chota Nagpore from a crowd of southern Dravidians. Even in parts of Bengal where such "Kolārian" folk have settled some generations ago, and have acquired the local language and dress, they are almost as easily distinguished as a Hindu undergraduate in Cambridge. If physical characters are rightly divided into "indefinite" signs of race, which can only be described with difficulty and hesitation in ordinary language, and the "definite" signs which can be measured and reduced to figures, yet the general aspect of a tribe or caste is the first thing which strikes an experienced enquirer's eye, and leads him to make further and more detailed investigations.

So is it also with those divisions, peculiar to India, which are known to us by the Portuguese name of *caste*. The Indian name for caste is *varna*, or "colour," and physical differences between different castes were fairly obvious even before accurate averages were struck between many individual measurements. Caste has undoubtedly tended, and for similar reasons, to perpetuate such differences between classes of men as we readily recognise between different breeds of horses or cattle. The ages of men succeed one another more slowly than the generations of domestic animals, and segregation, in spite of caste rules, has probably at no time been so rigid as in the case of pure-bred animals. But there is a restriction in the matter of marriage which has been more or less efficacious, and especially so in the case of the higher castes, where the women are more carefully guarded, and pride of birth influences the future mothers of the race. In some rare instances, castes are still racial, preserved from immixture by much the same feeling which leads the white American to protect his race from a mingling of Negro or Red Indian blood. Other castes are still recognisably the result and record of such forbidden mixtures. Sometimes the resulting difference is so great as to be visible in actual measurements. Often the result is a mere peculiarity of aspect, such as enables an expert to identify a mongrel or a crossbreed among domesticated animals. In any case, once a caste is formed, it is fenced in by matrimonial rules, strict in proportion to the social status and consideration of the group. Not only, then, are the racial origins of modern India more various than those of Europe, but such varieties of colour, stature, and culture as exist tend to be perpetuated.

It has been said, somewhat paradoxically, that whereas in Europe the divisions between races of men cut perpendicularly, as it were, so as to be more or less local and geographical, in India the separating lines run horizontally, and represent social strata. This, of course, is only partly true. The ancient Hindu theory of caste assumes the existence of four great divisions of Hindu humanity, extending all over India; namely, Brāhmans or priests, Kshatriyas, or warriors; Vaiçyas, or trading and professional folk; and Sūdras, who are most justly and aptly to be described as "the remainder." In all parts of Hindu India may be found representatives of this ancient and theoretical division of humanity, the first two usually claiming a western origin as eagerly as some of us claim a tincture of Norman blood. But it would be incorrect to say that even the highest and purest of these four divisions is of uniform race, or anything approaching to it, all over India. A Bengali Brāhman, for instance, can be more or less easily distinguished from other Bengalis, if he has the typical appearance of his caste. But he is even more easily distinguished from Brāhmans of other Provinces. How much of this last difference is due to mixture of blood, how much to difference of food and climate, it is, of course, difficult to say. But certainly caste produces a difference of breed in addition to the ethnical varieties of origin which differentiate the Indian populations from those of Europe.

Thirdly, some clue to Indian racial differences may be found in the religions of the peninsula. The greatest of these is still the Indian religion *par excellence*, the wonderful collection of varied speculations, beliefs, and practices known to us as Hinduism, and its daughter, the religion of Buddha. The latter has spread far and wide, has subjugated Ceylon and Burma, and is the leading religion of the Far East. At one time, it was supposed to be entirely or nearly extinct in India, although students had discovered traces of its influence in the Vishnuvite sects of Hinduism. Recent researches have shown that an almost unaltered form of Buddhism survives in the very bosom of Hinduism, and is practised under Hindu names among certain castes of Bengal and Orissa. It is to be noted that the investigations into these survivals have been for the most part conducted by Bengali Hindus, among whom is springing up a school of ethnologists and comparative linguists, who only need a better knowledge and understanding of European methods to be invaluable aids to western research in such matters. In Bengal, a work of purely anthropological interest has actually been published in the vernacular, an interesting account of the Chakmas, a Tibeto-Burman but partly Hinduised race on the eastern border of Bengal. Closely akin to the lower forms of Hinduism, and often subtly blending with them, are many Animistic religions, most of them professed by aboriginal tribes, speaking one or other of the aboriginal languages.

Islam and Christianity are, of course, imported and proselytising religions, and yield few if any clues to racial or social origins. Many Muhammadans profess to be, and not a few are, of authentic foreign origin. But during the seven hundred years of Muslim rule in India, there was much intermarriage with native races, and even more conversion. It is curious that, as in the case of Christianity, the conversions have been mostly among tribes and classes of the humbler sort. These were not denied admission into Hinduism, but they were only admitted on terms of social and racial degradation. Islam and Christianity alike claim to overlook the accidents of birth and status, and hence attract those to whom Hinduism only offered a place among the lowest ranks of its social hierarchy. But even in the case of the religions of Christ and Muhammad, the inveterate Indian tendency to recognise and insist on breed and social status has asserted itself again and again. Among Muhammadans, the Arabic tribal names have come to be the designations of social units which differ but little from the endogamous castes of Hinduism, and the same tendency is already evident among Christian converts. There is a marked reluctance in some quarters among ex-Hindus to intermarry with ex-Muslims, or even to participate in sacramental Communion with them.

As with caste, so with religion, the divisions are not strictly horizontal. As Christianity is not one thing all over Europe, but has differences of creed, ritual, and practice corresponding to racial differences, so the Hinduism, and even the Muhammadanism, of different provinces varies. There is no sharp boundary; there are elements in common wherever we go. But just as Dravidian temple architecture can be easily distinguished, even by the unpractised eye, from that of the edifices of the Gangetic plains, so local peculiarities of belief or ritual may come to the aid of the anthropologist, and may suggest or confirm distinctions more easily verified and more capable of scientific proof.

The study of all these matters is not without a practical and administrative interest at the present time. A hundred and fifty years ago, to the racial, tribal, and caste differences, accompanied by differences of language and religion, were added political divisions, accentuated by frequent dynastic or predatory wars. British rule has introduced two powerful unifying influences. Our system of administration, while it is adapted more or less effectively (more in some cases, less in others, according to the talent and character of local officers) to local precedents and local needs, is moulded by the great supervising and consolidating authority of the Governor-General in Council.

Secondly, higher education in India is conducted for the most part in English, and educated India, rapidly growing in numbers, has English for its second language, and is modifying local beliefs, usages, aspirations, patriotisms in accordance with ideas more or less consciously assimilated from European teachers and models. No one can deny that this new unity of India is the direct result of centralised British rule. In the far distance of time, all or nearly all India would, for a while, accept the domination of some Hindu ruler or dynasty. Under the Muhammadans, similarly, there were times when the Emperor at Delhi was the ruler of all or nearly all India. Under British rule, a much wider and more populous India, ranging from Baluchistan to Burma, and only excepting the semi-independent states which have been allowed to retain sovereign powers, is really and for the first time part of the greatest administration on earth except that of China, if we look to numbers. It is a result, as the history of British India shows, for which we cannot claim the whole credit. The direction of the great work of unification has been in British hands; it has chiefly been carried out by indigenous agency, and, in matters of detail, in deference to Indian ideas and Indian suggestions. Even fifty years ago, few Indians supposed that the wide Empire of India could be governed save under British guidance, or without the aid of British bayonets. The old habitual forces of disruption were too obvious; the distrust of one race for another was still too keenly felt to allow Indian politicians to imagine a united India under indigenous rule. But as the educated classes grow in power, in numbers, in self-reliance, and reliance on one another; as some of them are promoted to posts of higher trust and authority in India, and even in England, it is perhaps only natural that Indians should suppose that, so far as politics and administration are concerned, the old divisions and dissensions are obsolete, and that united India can in future be governed by native agency. That is not a matter with which ethnology has anything to do. It is the ethnologist's business merely to record impartially what racial, tribal, social, and religious differences still survive, and, if he can, to show how far they have been, and are being, obliterated by the spread of education, and by growing self-confidence and ambition among educated Indians. Whether the information the ethnologist collects can be put to any administrative use does not concern him, nor does he desire that his impartiality shall be affected by these considerations. But, in a little book of this kind it may not be amiss to point out that one result of British rule has been the growth of a new type of Indian, the educated Indian; who, whether he be Hindu or Muhammadan or Buddhist, is at least inclined to subordinate the old hereditary divisions to common political ambitions. These ambitions affect the fortunes and the future of some three hundred millions of humbler Indians, at present only linked by the accident of common British rule, and, so far as they are Hindus, by a common Hindu sentiment.

In the following chapters, it will be my business to tell, as briefly and clearly as possible, of (1) the Ethnology and Castes of the Indian Peoples; (2) the Languages of India; (3) the Religions of India. I hope what I have already said will sufficiently show why these three subjects are treated in this order.

PLATE I

Mahābrāhmans
(Mirzapur district)

Chapter I

Race and Caste

CURIOUSLY enough, the systematic enquiry into the physical race-characteristics of the Indian peoples was due to a daring assertion by Mr Nesfield, of the Indian Educational Service, to the effect that, so far as physical signs go, there is practically only one Indian race and one Indian caste. This was a hasty but quite natural generalisation from experience of a part of India, the United Provinces, which is in the heart of the Aryan settlement in the Gangetic *do-āb* (the area between "two rivers"). Here caste has long been a settled institution, and innumerable sub-castes, professional or the result of outcasting, have come into existence. Mr Nesfield was driven by his local observations to assert the unity of one great Indian race; he denied the truth of "the modern doctrine which divides the population of India into Aryan and aboriginal": he sturdily declared that it was impossible to distinguish a scavenger from a Brāhman, save by costume and other artificial and accidental marks. Even in the United Provinces this uncompromising statement awoke dissent. In other parts of India, as, for instance, on the north-eastern frontier, the crowded home of many races and languages, dissent was eager and loud. It was evident, on the face of it, that Mr Nesfield's new dogma was based on too limited a study. Caste, for him, was a mere matter of hereditary function and profession; since most castes in the sacred "midland" of Hinduism have assumed that guise. There is no reason to suppose that castes have usually or even often been formed as professional guilds. They come into being for many reasons, some of which will be presently stated; and in civilised communities, where the division of labour and specialisation of professional skill are well established, a caste gradually assumes some distinctive means of livelihood. But on the borders of Hinduism, where the Hindu social system is still assimilating new races, instances abound of racial castes, tribal castes, perhaps even (though this is a more doubtful matter) totemistic castes.

Those who had the widest experience of the Peninsula were convinced that its races were at least as varied as those of Europe: those who, like Mr Nesfield, had made a close study of one limited tract, might have continued to believe that under the superficial distinctions of caste and class lay a real unity of race. But Mr (afterwards Sir H. H.) Risley had spent the early years of his Indian service among the Dravidian tribes of Chota Nagpore, and was aware that they differ more widely from the people Mr Nesfield had studied than an Englishman differs from a Turk. The difference, indeed, was almost as great as that between a European and a Chinaman. Could such differences be registered and described in such a way as to convince minds accustomed to scientific accuracy in statement? Mr Risley thought he saw his way to an ethnological classification of Indian races and castes by means of the then comparatively new methods of anthropometry. In 1891, he published in the *Journal of the Anthropological Institute* a paper which marked the beginning of systematic ethnological studies in India. It contained a summary of the measurements of eighty-nine castes and tribes of Bengal, the United Provinces, and Bihār. It dealt, therefore, with the great alluvial plain, created by the Ganges and Indus, which lies between the Himalayas and the *massif central* of the Deccan. Here is the home of the Aryan immigrants, where the great Indo-European languages are spoken by communities as numerous as the larger European nations. Anthropometry showed in the plainest, the most incontrovertible way, that the caste system of marriages had sorted out men into classes possessing definite and recognisable physical characteristics. There were local differences, and caste differences. It only remained to extend anthropometrical measurements to other parts of India to prove that the many languages and religious beliefs of India are associated with an even greater variety of physical qualities. Such enquiries are still in progress, but many notable results have already been obtained, especially by Mr Edgar Thurston, in his now famous investigations into Dravidian ethnography.

The most important and significant measurement is that of the shape of the head. It is, of course, impossible to take a man at random and to say with certainty that the excessive length or breadth of his skull proves him to belong to a given race. But the average skull-measurements of a race are distinctive, and confirm, on the whole, the impressions created by general aspect, colour, language and other vaguer indications. The general result is as follows. At either end of the Himalayan range, in Baluchistan on the west, and in Assam and Burma on the east, broad heads prevail. Broad too are the heads of the mostly Mongolian races inhabiting the valleys of the southern slopes of the Himalayas, and in a belt of country running down the western coast at least as far south as Coorg. In the Panjāb, Rājputānā, and the United Provinces, tracts where the climate is dry and healthy, where great summer heat is compensated for by a bracing winter, where wheat is for the most part the staple food, long heads predominate. In Bihār, travelling eastwards, medium heads are most common. In the damp and steamy delta of Bengal, inhabited by over forty millions of rather dusky rice-eating people, there is a marked tendency towards the Mongolian brachy-cephaly of Tibeto-Burman races. It is visible among the Muhammadans and Chandāls of Eastern Bengal, people who are probably indigenous in this tract, it is more marked among the Kāyasthas, the writer-caste of Bengal, which claims a western and Aryan origin. It reaches its maximum development among the Bengali Brāhmans. South of the Vindhya mountains, where the population is chiefly Dravidian, with a comparatively small and ancient mixture of northern blood, the prevalent type is mainly long-headed or medium-headed. The coast-population has been much affected by foreign influences. On the east coast Malayan, Indo-Chinese and even Portuguese settlers have altered the local type. On the west coast, Arab, Persian, African, European, and Jewish immigrants have mingled with local races, and have changed their physiognomy, stature, and character of mind and body.

It is still a moot point, which the Mendelists may some day settle for us, whether head-form is a true hereditary race-characteristic, whether the osseous structure of the body generally is not a result of climate, food and other such circumstances of environment. Yet the shape of the head as shown by average measurements does mark off races of men which are separated by other differences than those of habitat. They do correspond to those vaguer yet unmistakeable characteristics which enable us to tell one race from another. The Mongolian, even when he settles in the plains of Assam, Bengal, or Burma and takes to a diet of rice and fish, keeps his round head and his smooth hairless face. The Aryan of the north-west has a markedly long head, which, in his case, goes with a fair complexion and luxuriant beard. The Dravidian, darkest of Indian races, with a tendency to crinkly or curly hair, has also a long or medium head. The mixed races of Bengal have, it is not surprising to find, medium heads, which tend in the upper castes to become broad.

Another significant index to race is the measurement of the nose. The results of nose-measurements roughly divide the peoples of India into three classes—those having narrow or fine noses (leptorrhine), in which the width is less than 70 per cent. of the height; those having medium noses (mesorrhine), with an average index of from 70 to 85; and broad-nosed (platyrrhine) people, the width of whose noses exceed 85 per cent. Here we get a physical means of distinguishing between the long-headed people of north-western India, fair and stalwart, and the almost equally long-headed dusky folk of the south. For the average nose of southern India, in Madras, the Central Provinces, and Chota Nagpore, is broad. In the Panjāb and Baluchistan we get fine noses of what, to us Europeans, seems an aristocratic type. In Afghanistan, noses are so long and hooked as to give the tall and vigorous Afghan a Jewish aspect. In the rest of India, and especially down the west coast, noses are of medium type. A still more interesting discovery is the fact that anywhere outside the Aryan tracts of the north-west, the broad nose is a distinct sign of aboriginal blood. In Bengal, for instance, the lower castes have broad noses. The priestly and writer castes, for all their broad heads, have fine noses, which support their claim to a western origin. Roughly speaking, the broad nose goes with primitive forms of social organisation, with totemistic exogamous clans. Finer noses are usually associated with communities of a more modern type; and above these again come social units, castes and tribes, which claim descent from eponymous saints and heroes.

A third physical measurement enables us to effect a further sorting out of Indian races. What is called the "flatness" of the Mongolian face is plain to the most careless observer. This is due chiefly to the formation of the cheekbone, and its relation to the socket of the eye and the root of the nose. This can be measured and expressed in figures, with the result that the Mongoloid people of the north-east and the Himalayan region can be definitely distinguished from the broad-headed races of Baluchistan, Bombay, and Coorg.

Finally, it is possible to arrive at the average stature of various Indian races and communities. The tallest races are found in the north-west, in Baluchistan, the Panjāb and Rājputānā. A progressive diminution is seen as we go down the valley of the Ganges, until we find very short folk among the Assam hill tribes. The Dravidians of the south are shorter than the Aryans of the north. The smallest Indian tribe is that of the Negritos of the Andaman Islands, whose average height is only 4 feet 10½ inches.

From a careful comparison of these measurements, Sir Herbert Risley arrived at the classification of Indian humanity, which, for the moment, is the accepted division, into seven main physical types. Beginning with the north-western frontier, these are as follows:—

(1) The *Turko-Iranian* type, which comprises the Baloches, Brāhuis and Afghans of Baluchistan and the north-west Frontier Province. These are probably the result of a fusion of Turkī and Persian blood, and are all Muhammadans. The general aspect is wholly different from that of other Indian races, and no one who has ever seen an Afghan or Baloch, with his long Jewish nose and plentiful hair and beard, can ever confuse this type with any other. In temperament also these men of the border differ from other Indians. They are a fierce and warlike race, engaged in constant blood-feuds with one another.

(2) The *Indo-Aryan* type, with its home in the Panjāb, Rājputānā and Kashmir, has as its most conspicuous members the Rājputs, Khattris and Jāts. These, in all but colour (and even in colour they are hardly more dusky than the races round the Mediterranean) closely resemble the well-bred European in type. In stature they are tall, their complexion is fair; "eyes dark; hair on face plentiful; head long; nose narrow and prominent, but not

specially long." One significant peculiarity of this group is that there is little difference in physical character between the upper and lower classes. This, as we shall presently see, is what we should expect from what is known of the history of these peoples. The upper social ranks probably represent the blood, but little diluted with indigenous mixture, of the Aryan immigrants. Even in the lower classes, the typical Aryan characteristics are now so prominent that any indigenous strain that exists is no longer noticeable in average measurements. Only in height, a quality especially sensitive to differences of food and sanitation, are the lower castes inferior. Here we get a remarkable modern instance of transformation of type. The preaching of the Sikh reformers, involving a change of food and the inculcation of martial discipline and fervour, has converted the despised scavenging Chuhrā into the soldierly Mazhabi, once a redoubtable foe of the English, and now one of the finest soldiers in the British army.

(3) The *Scytho-Dravidian* type, including the Marāthā Brāhmans, the Kunbīs, and the Coorgs of western India. These peoples differ from the Turko-Iranian races in being shorter, in having longer heads, higher noses, and flatter faces.

(4) The *Aryo-Dravidian* or Hindostāni type, which exists in the United Provinces, in parts of Rājputānā, and in Bihār. This type appears to be due to a mixture of Indo-Aryan and Dravidian strains. The higher classes resemble Indo-Aryans, the lower have a distinctly Dravidian aspect. Yet, even to the eye, they form a type apart and are easily recognised. In this type, the average nose-index corresponds exactly to social status. The noses grow broader as we go downwards in the social scale.

(5) The very interesting *Mongolo-Dravidian* or *Bengali* type which is found in Bengal and Orissa. Here Aryan influences may still be detected in the upper classes, but there has been extensive mingling with Tibeto-Burman and Dravidian peoples, and other aboriginal inhabitants. The main distinguishing feature is the broad head, which is most conspicuous in the upper classes. It is shared equally by the Bengali Brāhman, who claims a western origin, and the Chittagong Mag, whose Tibeto-Burman origin is not denied. The Brāhman, on the other hand, inherits a fine and narrow nose,

which may very well be due to Indo-Aryan ancestry. Recent investigations tend to show that Buddhism survived till a comparatively recent date in Bengal. Hence, no doubt, a temporary disregard of caste restrictions and a freer mixture with local strains.

(6) The *Mongoloid* type of the Himalayas, Nepāl, Assam, and Burma. "The head is broad: complexion dark, with a yellowish tinge; hair on face scanty; stature short or below average; nose fine to broad; face characteristically flat; eyelids often oblique." Here we have races which, if somewhat dark, correspond to the ideas most of us entertain about the external aspect and temperament of the Siamese or Japanese. In intellectual ability, and what we may call the artistic faculty, they are inferior to the Bengali. Most Europeans, however (or is it, therefore?) find them among the most congenial of Indian races. They are social, good-natured, straightforward people. In the western Himalayas, there has been intermixture with Aryan invaders, as in the Kangra Valley and Nepāl, and the ruling dynasties claim Rājput origin, for the Indo-Aryans loved to settle in the cool hills, much as the Anglo-Indian does to this day. But on the mountainous frontiers of North-East Bengal and Assam, the Mongoloid peoples have remained undisturbed till our own time. Linguistically, this group is peculiarly interesting, since they speak many tongues, many of which still remain to be recorded and studied by European scholars.

(7) The *Dravidian* type, which extends from Ceylon to the valley of the Ganges and covers all South-Eastern India. It is found in Madras, Hyderabad, the Central Provinces, most of Central India, and Chota Nagpore. Its purest representatives dwell on the Malabar coast and in Chota Nagpore. Here we have probably the original inhabitants of India, now modified in some degree by an infiltration of Aryan, Scythian and Mongoloid elements. "The stature is short or below mean; the complexion very dark, approaching black; hair plentiful, with an occasional tendency to curl; eyes dark; head long; nose very broad, sometimes depressed at the root, but not so as to make the face appear flat."

PLATE II

Kāyasthas—the writer caste
(Mirzapur district)

It must, of course, be understood, that these types and the names allotted to them merely show that in certain areas the average characteristics of the peoples dwelling there can be sufficiently separated to be recognisable not only by eye but by the callipers of the anthropologist. The names, it will be noticed, in some cases, imply theories as to the origin of the races thus grouped together. These theories are partly based on measurements, partly on tradition, partly on linguistic considerations. It remains for me to state, very rapidly, what these theories are.

That the Dravidians are the oldest race in India is rendered *primâ facie* probable by the fact that they inhabit the southernmost part of the peninsula, between races who can with some certainty be called invaders—and the deep sea. There is a remarkable uniformity of physical characteristics among the lower specimens of this type. They have in common an animistic religion, their distinctive language, their peculiar stone monuments, and a primitive system of totemism. They do not resemble Europeans on the one hand, or the races of the Far East on the other. Until proof to the contrary is forthcoming they may well be regarded as the autochthones of India.

There is more room for difference of opinion as to the origins of the brilliant and highly civilised Indo-Aryans of the Panjāb and Rājputānā. As I have said before, we have here a population closely resembling that of modern Europe in many respects. I might have added that it still more closely resembles the Europe of the Roman empire. Nowhere else in Hindu India does caste sit so lightly, or approach so nearly to the social classes of Europe. Though there are rules, or rather customs, forbidding intermarriage between different castes, yet these are mitigated by the custom, not unknown to ourselves, of *hypergamy*. This simply means that a man may take a wife from a lower caste, but will not give his daughters to men of that caste. The result is a uniformity of physical type found nowhere else in India. Moreover these people speak a language of the Indo-European family, and have many words and idioms in common with ourselves. The present theory of their origin is simply that they are in the bulk immigrants into India, immigrants who came into the land from the north-west with their herds and families, as the Jews entered into and possessed Palestine.

One chief objection to this theory is that the lands through which they must have passed are in no way fitted to be an *officina gentium*, being now dry, barren, and all but deserted. But abundant indications remain to show that the climate of South-Eastern Persia and the tracts to the north has changed within comparatively recent times. The relics of crowded populations and ancient civilisations abound in regions now sandy desert, and there is evidence in the tales told by Greek and Chinese travellers that the Panjāb itself, most of it comparatively arid, was once well wooded. The theory then is that the homogeneous and handsome population of the Panjāb and Rājputānā represents the almost pure descendants of Aryan settlers, who carried the Indo-European languages now prevailing over Northern India, just as our own emigrants took the English language to America.

But we have also to account for the Aryo-Dravidians who inhabit the sacred "midland" country of Hinduism, and here we have Dr Hoernle's now famous theory, remarkably confirmed by the researches of Sir George Grierson's *Linguistic Survey*. This theory supposes that a second swarm of Aryan-speaking people, perhaps driven forward by the change of climate in central Asia, entered India through the high and difficult passes of Gilgit and Chitral, and established themselves in the fertile plains between the Ganges and the Jumna. They followed a route which made it impossible for their women to accompany them. They took to themselves wives from the daughters of dusky Dravidian aborigines. Here, by contact with a different, and in their sentiment, inferior race, caste came into being. Here most of the Vedic hymns were composed. Here, by a blending of imported and indigenous religious ideals, the ritual and usages of Hindu religion came into being, to spread in altered forms east and west and south. The necessity for this second hypothesis is twofold. It accounts for the marked ethnical barrier which separates western from eastern Hindustan. Elsewhere the various types melt imperceptibly into one another. Here alone is a definite racial border line. Again, the theory accounts for the fact that the Vedic hymns contain no description whatever of the earlier Aryan migration, and for the fact that the inhabitants of the middle land always felt a dislike for the early immigrants as men of low culture and barbarous manners. For the present, at all events, and perhaps for all time, Dr Hoernle's ingenious theory holds the field.

No special theory is required to account for the physical and mental qualities of the Mongolo-Dravidians of Bengal. No doubt the original population was Dravidian with a strong intermixture of Tibeto-Burmese blood, especially in the east and north-east. But the Hindu religion, developed in the sacred Midlands round Benares, spread to Bengal, bringing with it the Indo-European speech which in medieval times became the copious and supple Bengali tongue. From the west too came what we in Europe would call the gentry, the priestly and professional castes. These have acquired most of the local physical characters, dusky skin, low stature, round heads. But in nearly all cases, the fineness and sharp outline of the nose shows their aristocratic origin, and in some instances a Bengali Brāhman has all the physical distinction of a western priest or sage.

When we turn to the Scytho-Dravidian group we have again to fall back on records of ancient invasions from the north. Ancient some of them were, but far less ancient than the settlement of the Aryans in the north-west. The Sakas have provided India with one of its many chronological eras; they founded dynasties which have left coins behind them, they have left vague but widely spread traditions. They were what we Europeans call Scythians. They were known to the Persians, the Parthians, and the Chinese. Their original home seems to have been in the south of China, a land of pre-eminently round-headed races. We know that they established their dominion over portions of the Panjāb, Sind, Gujarāt, Rājputānā and Central India. If they have left traces of their settlement on their descendants we may reasonably expect to find round-headed races and tribes in regions mostly surrounded by long-headed peoples. Such a zone of broad-headed people does in fact extend from the western Panjāb right through the Deccan, till it finally ends in Coorg. Sir H. H. Risley's theory is that the Scythians first occupied the great grazing country of the western Panjāb, and finding their progress eastwards blocked by the Indo-Aryans, turned southwards, mingled with the Dravidians, and became the ancestors of the warlike Marātha race. Such an origin forms a tempting explanation of the well-known predatory habits of the Marātha hordes, and of their frequent raids all over the peninsula under the decaying administration of the later Mogul Emperors. It is an interesting and fascinating speculation, since it accounts not only for the physical aspect of the Marāthas but for their characteristic political genius, for their wide-ranging forays, their guerilla warfare, their unscrupulous dealings, their inveterate love of intrigue, their clannish habits.

I must here boldly borrow Sir H. H. Risley's summary of the historical record of Scythian invasions into India, since that is the main justification for his theory. "In the time of the Achaemenian kings of Persia," he says, "the Scythians, who were known to the Chinese as Sse, occupied the regions lying between the lower course of the Sillis or Jaxartes and Lake Balkash. The fragments of early Scythian history which may be collected from classical writers are supplemented by the Chinese annals, which tell us how the Sse, originally located in southern China, occupied Sogdiana and Trans-oxiana at the time of the establishment of the Graeco-Bactrian monarchy. Dislodged from these regions by the Yueh-chi, who had themselves been put to flight by the Huns, the Sse invaded Bactriana, an enterprise in which they were frequently allied with thc Parthians. To this circumstance, Ujfalvy says may be due the resemblance which exists between the Scythian coins of India and those of the Parthian kings. At a later period, the Yueh-chi made a further advance, and drove the Sse or Sakas out of Bactriana, whereupon the latter crossed the Paropamisus and took possession of the country called after them Sakastān, comprising Segistān, Arachosia, and Drangiana. But they were left in possession only for a hundred years, for about 25 B.C. the Yueh-chi disturbed them afresh. A body of Scythians then emigrated eastwards, and founded a kingdom in the western portion of the Panjāb. The route they followed in their advance upon India is uncertain; but to a people of their habits it would seem that a march through Baluchistan would have presented no serious difficulties.

"The Yueh-chi, afterwards known as the Tokhari, were a power in Central Asia and the north-west of India for more than five centuries, from 130 B.C. The Hindus called them Sakas and Turushkas, but their kings seem to have known no other dynastic title than that of Kushan. The Chinese annals tell us how Kitolo, chief of the Little Kushans, whose name is identified with the Kidara of the coins, giving way before the incursion of the Ephthalites, crossed the Paropamisus, and founded, in the year 425 of our era, the kingdom of Gandhāra, of which, in the time of his son, Peshawar became the capital. About the same time, the Ephthalites or Ye-tha-i-li-to of the Chinese annals, driven out of their territory by the Yuan-yuan, started westward, and overran in succession Sogdiana, Khwarizan (Khiva), Bactriana, and finally the north-west portion of India. Their movements reached India in the reign of Skanda Gupta (452-80) and brought about the disruption of the Gupta empire. The Ephthalites were known in India as Huns. The leader of the invasion of India, who succeeded in snatching Gandhāra from the Kushans and established his capital at Sākala, is called by the Chinese Laelih, and inscriptions enable us to identify him with the original Lakhan Udayāditya of the coins. His son Toramāna (490-515) took possession of Gujarāt, Rājputānā, and part of the Ganges valley, and in this way the Huns acquired a portion of the ancient Gupta kingdom. Toramāna's successor, Mihirakula (515-44), eventually succumbed to the combined attack of the Hindu princes of Mālwā and Magadha."

I now come to the ethnography as distinguished from the ethnology of India. Of anthropometry and the lessons to be learnt from it, I have no personal experience, and have had to borrow my materials at second-hand. But with the great system of caste, its workings, its manifold ramifications, everyone who has lived in India has come into more or less close contact. How important caste is in the social life of the country may be easily inferred from this little fact. I once asked the late Navin Chandra Sen, then the most popular of Bengali poets, if he would attempt a definition of what a Hindu is. After many suggestions, all of which had to be abandoned on closer examination, the poet came to the conclusion that a Hindu is (1) one who is born in India of Indian parents on both sides, and (2) accepts and obeys the rules of caste. Hinduism is, roughly speaking, the religion of the Aryo-Dravidians, the upper and fairer classes among whom regarded the aborigines, matrimonially, much as white Americans regard their negro fellow citizens. It has spread over nearly the whole of India and is still spreading, usually but not always, carrying with it one of the Indo-European languages of India. It is the religion and social system of races and classes which consider themselves intrinsically superior, and practise a traditional kind of eugenics, of race preservation. Humbler or more barbarous races are admitted on various conditions into caste, sometimes into higher, sometimes into lower positions. The process is one of that kind of "legal fiction" with which students of Roman law are familiar. It is a process of unification and, at the same time, of social segregation. I have already alluded to the suggestion that caste-divisions are horizontal, as it were, compared with the geographical divisions of races. But it is always dangerous to make general statements about three hundred millions of people scattered over so large an area as India. There are Brāhmans in every part of India, and these usually trace their origin back to the sacred midland where Hinduism came into being. They may be, and probably are, the descendants of the missionaries by whom the religion of the Hindus is, imperceptibly and without open proselytism, spread abroad. Something corresponding to a warrior caste and a caste of scribes is to be found in most provinces, and many of these either claim to be migrants, or have been admitted by adoption into the privileges of warrior or writer blood.

But there are many castes which are purely local, even in name, and are not found elsewhere than in the places where they were admitted into the Hindu community. Many closely printed pages in the Census Reports of each province and state enumerate and describe the thousands of castes revealed by the numbering of the people. It is, of course, only possible to give a very vague and general idea of some of the classes into which the castes of India may conveniently be divided.

I am tempted here to borrow Sir Herbert Risley's definition of caste. But it is a highly abstract definition, and one that cannot be easily carried in the head, even by those who have a practical and familiar acquaintance with members of Indian castes. Roughly a caste is a group of human beings who may not intermarry, or (usually) eat, with members of any other caste. There are also sub-castes which are also endogamous. Very frequently, especially in the parts of India where caste is already an institution of immemorial antiquity, a caste has allotted to it a profession or occupation.

Before we discuss castes properly so called, it is convenient to speak of the tribes of India, since tribes have a tendency to become castes when they come under the pervasive influence of Hindu social ideas. In the south of India are Dravidian tribes, of which the best example are the tribes of Chota Nagpore. These are divided into a number of exogamous groups or clans, calling themselves by the name of an animal or plant, which may be regarded as their totem. The Khonds of Orissa, who once bore an evil name for their practice of human sacrifices to propitiate the earth-goddess, are divided into fifty *gochis* or exogamous clans, each of which bears the name of a village, and believes itself to be descended from a common ancestor. These *gochis* are the nearest known approach to the local exogamous tribe which Mr McLennan and the French sociologists believe to be the earliest form of human society.

The Mongoloid tribes of Assam are much of the same kind, but in many cases, as among the head-hunting Nagas, live at perpetual warfare with one another. In such cases they usually capture their wives in war. It is interesting to note that when population grows too dense for the profitable pursuit of the chase, their principal means of livelihood, such a tribe breaks up into two or more "villages," which immediately begin waging war with one another, which is quite what a French sociologist would expect them to do. I can tell of a case within my own experience in which the headman of a parent village invited the chief of a colony village (his own nephew) to a feast and palaver with his young warriors. The guests were all treacherously put to the sword, as a means of acquiring heads and concubines. I could not get the headman to see that he had been guilty of an atrocious crime. For him, it was lawful strategy. And indeed Naga warfare is merely a series of artfully planned ambushes in which not a few of our own officers perished before we undertook the direct administration of the Naga Hills. Sir H. Risley remarks of this group of tribes that "no very clear traces of totemism have been discovered among them." Subsequent enquiries, however, show that totemistic clans do exist in some of the Assam tribes.

Of the Turko-Iranian tribes of the north-western frontier I need not speak at any length, since these tribes are all sturdy followers of the Prophet, and save that they are under British rule can hardly be said to belong to India at all. There is no likelihood that they will ever be received into the tolerant bosom of Hinduism, since, to the Indian proper, the Baloch and the Afghan are disagreeable and swaggering caterans, who have an innate scorn for the typical Hindu hierarchy of caste. Among these tribes it is martial ability and valour that win a man consideration and wives.

Let us now turn to caste properly so called, the traditional social divisions of the Hindus. And first it is necessary to say something of the ancient Hindu theory of what caste is, and how it came into existence.

As with the Hebrews, the religious literature of India contains a vast mass of what can only be called law, and perhaps, the most famous of Indian law books is the Institutes of Manu, a compilation of rules relating to magic, religion, law, custom, ritual and metaphysics. Even to this day, these branches of speculation and enquiry, so distinct to western imaginations, are apt to be confused together as a result of the pantheistic feeling which pervades Hinduism. The Institutes is a comparatively modern book, but it repeats ideas which are found in a more or less explicit form in early authorities[1]. In this book we are told that in the beginning of things the Pan-theos who "contains all created things and is inconceivable" produced by effort of thought a golden egg, from which he himself was born as Brahmā, the creator of the known universe. From his mouth, his arms, his thighs, and his feet respectively he created the four great leading castes, the Brāhman, the Kshatriya, the Vaiçya, and the Sūdra. These were, briefly, the priests, the warriors and gentlefolk, the traders, and the servile classes of human society. The other castes were gradually formed, the theory states, by intermarriages between these. The three higher castes were allowed to take wives from lower castes. When the caste of the mother was next below that of the father, the child took the caste of his mother and no new caste was formed. But where the difference of condition was greater than this, new castes were formed, lower than those of either parent. Some discrepancies of rank produced unions which were regarded as peculiarly offensive to human feelings and as tantamount to incestuous intercourse. These resulted in very degraded castes. Where the father married beneath him, the marriage was described as *anuloma* or "with the hair." When a woman was guilty of a *mésalliance*, the marriage was called *pratiloma* or "against the hair." The most disgraceful union of this kind was that between a Brāhman woman and a Sūdra man, the resulting offspring being relegated to the caste of Chandāl. The unfortunate Chandāl is described as "that lowest of mortals," and is condemned, as Sir H. Risley says, to live outside the village, to clothe

[1] The actual date is very uncertain. Dr Burnell thinks the book was composed so late as A.D. 500, but it was probably much older.

himself in the garments of the dead, to eat from broken dishes, to execute criminals, and to carry out the corpses of friendless men.

The most superficial acquaintance with existing caste divisions shows that this theory is not so much a hypothesis as a fanciful fiction. In eastern Bengal, for instance, the Chandāl is evidently a Mongoloid aboriginal, with a considerable strain of Dravidian and perhaps even of Aryan blood. Yet the fiction shows plainly enough the estimation in which one of the numerically largest divisions of local society is held. Some thirty years ago, when I was a young magistrate, a comely Chandāl girl appeared before me, her face streaming with blood from a scalp wound. She asserted gravely that a Sūdra of higher caste had struck her on the head with a stick, because he had found her reading a book as she sat in the doorway of her father's cottage. I was disinclined to believe this story, but her assailant was promptly sent for, and being brought straight to me, admitted the truth of the charge, and seemed surprised at my indignation at a cowardly assault.

As an attempt to account for the origin and explain the nature of caste the theory of Manu is obviously a failure. But it contains a picture of the early castes. It is also interesting because the idea of four original *varnas* or "colours" of men may have been borrowed from the old Persian social organisation. The early scriptures, the Vedas, show that this conception of four original castes was not brought to India by Aryan immigrants. But when caste came into being as a result of the contact of Aryan settlers with Dravidian aborigines, this mythological explanation, which gave such conspicuous eminence to priests and warriors, an eminence already conceded to them on account of the importance of their functions, was readily accepted as a convincing explanation of the hereditary differences between men in society, a difference not merely of function, but of colour, aspect, gesture, speech, breeding, and intelligence. It is necessary to mention this theory, however briefly, since it still holds ground, except among those Indians who have had a European education and even among them has the interest of early and sacred associations which, in Europe, belongs to the cosmological speculations of the book of Genesis.

PLATE III

Dharkārs
(Mirzapur district)

What, next, are castes as they appear to the eye of the European ethnologist, free from preconceived prejudice, and only anxious to come as near the truth as is possible in his dealings with ancient institutions round which has gathered a vast mass of venerable superstition and religious speculation? In the first place, castes are often still recognisably *tribes*. Sometimes the leading men of an aboriginal tribe will acquire sufficient wealth and social consideration to wish to obtain the stamp of recognition as reputable Hindus. They will call themselves, for example, and induce their neighbours and the priests of these to call them, Rājputs. They may not at first succeed in intermarrying with true hereditary Rājputs, but in time they will be just Rājputs like any other Rājputs. Or, again, a number of non-Hindus, animists, will join one of the many Hindu sects or fraternities and will intermarry with Vaishnavas, Lingayats, Rāmayats, or other devotees of some favourite deity. Or again, a whole tribe or a considerable portion of a tribe, usually one of some political importance, will enter Hinduism by means of some plausible fiction. The instance quoted by Sir H. Risley is that of the Koches of north-eastern Bengal. These people are Tibeto-Burmans and until recent times spoke a dialect of the agglutinative Bodo language. They now call themselves Rājbansis, "of royal birth," or Bhāngā Kshatriyas, "broken warriors," names which enable them to claim an origin from the traditional dispersion of the Aryan warrior caste by the hero Parasu Rāma, "Rāma of the battle axe." They claim descent from the epic monarch Dasarath, father of Rāma, have their own Brāhmins, and have begun to adopt the Brāhminical system of exogamous *gotras*. But, as Sir H. Risley remarks, they are in a transitional state, since they have all hit upon the same *gotra*, and are therefore compelled to marry within it, except in the rare instances in which they contract unions with Bengali women.

A still more interesting, because more recent, instance of this sort is that of the Meithei, now known to Hindus as Manipuris. In the Mahābhārata is told the tale of how the hero Arjuna wandered from his brethren into Southern and Eastern India, and, among other adventures, met (as Æneas with Dido) with Chitrangadā, the fair daughter of the King of Manipur, somewhere near the eastern coast. Some 150 years ago, the then king of the beautiful valley of Imphāl, between Assam and Burma, was thinking of becoming a Muhammadan, by way of courting the favour of the Muhammadan rulers of Bengal. But Hindu priests persuaded him that a better way of linking his fortunes with those of India, rather than with Ava (with whose royal family his dynasty had usually intermarried), was by becoming Hindu with all his people. Imphāl was identified with Manipur, and many of the Meithei race became Vishnuvite Hindus with their ruler, though they retain their primitive Tibeto-Burman language. I may mention a little personal reminiscence to show how completely the change by fictitious adoption was accepted in Bengal. In 1891, my old friend and chief, Mr Quinton, with all his staff, was treacherously murdered at Manipur. Subsequently when I was magistrate of Chittagong, I found that my head clerk, an extremely mild and intelligent Bengali Kāyastha, had celebrated the easily suppressed mutiny at Manipur by writing a drama based on the ancient legend of Arjuna's amours with Chitrangadā!

Sometimes an aboriginal tribe will become a Hindu caste without losing its old tribal designation. They will worship Hindu gods without daring wholly to neglect tribal deities, which, as might perhaps be expected, are left chiefly to the women of the tribe. Such a tribe will rapidly assimilate itself to the beliefs and practices of Hindu neighbours, and finally only its name and (except in case of occasional intermarriage with other castes) its physical aspect will remain to testify to its origin.

Castes are at present classified as follows:

(1) What Sir H. Risley calls *the tribal type*, instances of which have been given above. Such tribal castes abound in all parts of India. It is not improbable that the great Sūdra division of Hindu tradition was originally the whole mass of Dravidian aboriginals as they came into contact with Aryan immigrants, and were conceded a subordinate place in their social system. It would be useless to give a list of the names of such castes, but I cannot refrain from mentioning the excellent Doms of the Assam Valley, whose name unfortunately associates them with very different people in India proper. They are obviously of Tibeto-Burman origin, and deserve closer study than they receive. Their long thatched places of worship, true synagogues for meeting together and curiously unlike the tiny *cellæ* of Hindu temples, are among the most conspicuous features of Assam villages.

They have no idols, and place a *puthi*, a holy book, on what may pass for the village altar. They are vaguely Hinduised, but will humbly declare "*āmi hindu na hô*," "we are not Hindu folk." Yet they are well on their way towards acceptance into caste, and have already a strong infusion of Hindu blood.

Other border races, though they are still too savage and independent to become Hindu, are marked down for absorption. Such, for instance, are the Daflas of the northern border of Assam, cousins of the Abors to whom attention has been drawn by recent events. The Daflas are still frankly animistic; their love of strong spirits and other intoxicants, their addiction to their favourite diet of roast pork, their extremely uncleanly habits and barbarous speech, all make them very offensive to the gentle vegetarian Hindus their neighbours. But it happens that the tribal costume closely resembles the traditional dress of Mahādēva, the Destroyer, the most active and formidable member of the Hindu Trinity, and already some Hindus speak of these genial Highlanders as Siva-bansa, as "of Siva's race." Many other examples, with interesting details of fictional methods, will be found in Mr E. A. Gait's admirable *History of Assam*.

(2) *The functional or occupational type* of caste. This is the form of caste best known to Europeans, because, since the first European missionaries and traders visited those parts of India where the caste system has had the longest opportunity to evolve, they came most into contact with this, which is probably the oldest and most elaborated form of caste. The Hindu theory of caste encouraged the adoption of special occupations, and now the evolution has proceeded so far that change of occupation may usually result in a change of caste. A remarkable instance of this is found in the Marāthi districts of the Central Provinces. Here is a separate and newly formed caste of village servants called Gārpagāri, "hail-averters," whose business it is to protect the village crops from hailstorms. Shepherds who take to tillage break away from their pastoral brethren, and so on. Even those who retain their traditional occupations are wont to adopt more seemly-sounding names than those that belong to their trade. I have known barbers who called themselves Chandra-vaidyas[2], which is a promotion more subtle

[2] "Moon-physicians," an allusion to the crescent-shaped brass basin of the barber,

than a mere ascent to the status of "hair-dresser," and washermen who have followed suit by dubbing themselves Sukla-vaidya, a word of which "white-worker" is a crude but sufficiently suggestive translation.

(3) The *sectarian type* is a singularly interesting example of the strong social influence of Hindu sentiment. Nearly all new Hindu sects begin by renouncing caste in the enthusiastic following of some single deity, some new explanation of the mysteries of life, and love, and death. These sects are usually the followers of some reforming theorist, whose leadership is apt to become hereditary. Such sects almost always believe that all men are equal, or at all events, that all who accept their doctrines are equal. One of my most interesting recollections is of a now distant interview with a buxom middle-aged lady, the hereditary leader of the Kartā-bhajās of Central Bengal. She sat unveiled, and was accessible to all who, like myself, were interested in the community over which she exercised a firm but good-natured control. It is a picturesque detail that her chosen seat when receiving visitors was an ancient European four-poster bedstead. Her followers (and revenues) were growing rapidly, increased chiefly by the democratic instinct which, even in India, revolts against social prestige. But it would seem that when such a sect grows and spreads, the old separatist ideas reassert themselves, and the sect breaks up into smaller endogamous communities, whose status depends on the original position of the members in Hinduism. The most remarkable instance of this kind is furnished by the great Lingayat caste of Bombay, which contains over two and a half millions of members. In the twelfth century the Lingayats were a sect who believed in the equality of all men. In Mr P. J. Mead's Bombay Census Report for 1911 is a very interesting account of the present condition of the Lingayats, an account which shows how the scholar, the linguist, and the administrator can work together to find materials for the anthropologist. Dr Fleet's examination of ancient inscriptions has thrown much light on the origin of the sect, but the author of the Report holds that there may be some reason to think that the sect is much older than is commonly supposed. In any case, they are already divided into three great groups, comprising many subdivisions.

---

such as the helmet of Don Quixote, familiar to us all.

(4) *Castes formed by crossing* come aptly to show that there was some basis for Manu's theory of caste after all. Castes, nowadays, increase by fission, by throwing off sub-castes, and one species of these sub-castes is created by mixed marriages. This tendency, curiously enough, is most evident in Dravidian tribes, such as the Mundās, which are not yet wholly Hinduised, but have been affected by Hindu example. So far as I know, these mixed castes do not occur among the Mongoloid peoples, and I have come across cases where a member of an aboriginal tribe has been accepted into the caste of a Hindu girl he has married. In one case, within my own experience, the bridegroom had begun as an animist, had become Christian, and finally entered by marriage into the quite respectable Koch caste. One interesting caste in Bengal, that of the Shāgirdpeshas, owes its origin to concubinage with the so-called slaves, the women of tenants surrounding a homestead who pay their rent in service. This, it will be observed, is a caste of illegitimacy, in which the relationship between the legitimate and illegitimate children of a man of good caste is recognised, but the two are not allowed to eat together. The classical instance of a mixed caste is the Khas of Nepāl, said to be the result of very ancient intermarriages between Rājput or Brāhman immigrants and the Mongolian "daughters of men."

(5) *Castes of the national type.* This somewhat daring title we owe to the great authority of Sir H. Risley. As one instance, he mentions the Newārs, a Mongoloid people, who were once the ruling race in Nepāl, till the Gurkha invasion in 1769, and have now become a caste. Other instances might be found on the north-eastern frontier. But the people Sir Herbert Risley had in mind when he invented this term was undoubtedly the remarkable Marātha race, once the most daring warriors and freebooters in India, and now the rivals of the Bengalis in intellectual ability, and probably more than their equals in political sagacity. Sir Rāmkrishna Gopāl Bhandārkar is our authority for the statement that the Rattas were a tribe who held political supremacy in the Deccan from the earliest days. In time they became Mahā-rattas, "Great Rattas," and the land in which they lived was called Mahārattha, which, by a common linguistic habit of mankind, was Sanskritised into Mahā-rāshtra. Their marriage customs show marked traces of totemistic institutions. An extremely interesting account of the present condition of this warlike and enterprising race will be found at pp. 289, 290

of the Bombay Census Report for 1911. It neither supports nor discourages Sir H. Risley's ingenious theory of the Scythic origin of the Marāthas, which is at least a theory which recognises the respect in which our ancestors held their martial prowess and talents[3].

(6) *Castes formed by migration.* These are new castes which serve to enforce the warning against a too ready acceptance of the definition of caste as a "horizontal" division of humanity. It is a method of forming new communities of Hindus which is very easily intelligible to us, seeing that our own race is split into sections only differing from castes in not being strictly endogamous, such as Anglo-Indians, Australians, New Zealanders, and so forth. Members leave home and settle among strangers. They are assumed to have formed foreign habits, eaten strange food, worshipped alien gods, and have a difficulty—an expensive difficulty—in finding wives in the parent caste. After a time they marry only among themselves, become a sub-caste, and are often known by some territorial name, Bārendra, Rārhi, or what not. Such seemingly are the remarkable Nāmbudri Brāhmans of Malabar, and the Rārhi Brāhmans of Bengal. Sometimes change of habitat brings about loss of rank, sometimes promotion. These are matters on which the Census Reports now being published are full of interesting details. But they are matters which are not easily summarised. No doubt Mr Gait's Report on the combined results of Census operations in India will show the progress of castes of this type during the last ten years.

(7) *Castes formed by changes of custom.* This is a fruitful cause of new divisions of Hindu society. It is, for the moment, more than usually operative, owing to the spread of education, and often represents a difference of social opinion which corresponds, more or less closely, to Conservative and Radical ideas among ourselves. It evidently was always a cause of fissiparous tendencies. The most notable instance is the distinction between Jāts and Rājputs, both apparently sprung from the same stock, but separated socially, amongst other causes, by the fact that the former practise and the latter abjure infant marriages.

[3] But see the postscript to this chapter.

PLATE IV

Banjara women
(Mirzapur district)

This is a very rapid and highly summarised account of the races and castes of India. There are many obvious omissions. Nothing has been said of the Sikhs, little or nothing about the numerous races of the north-eastern frontier. But enough has been said to give a fair general impression of what the physical characters of the Indian peoples are, and what kind of institution caste is in its practical working. More might have been said about totemistic clans, but on this subject those who would pursue their studies further have only to turn to Dr J. G. Frazer's work on the subject. In the next chapter, I have to borrow my materials from Sir G. A. Grierson, and show how the peoples of India are divided by differences of language. On the whole, those linguistic divisions correspond with remarkable accuracy to the orographical and climatic structure of the country and the racial divisions which we owe to the learning and ingenuity of Sir H. H. Risley. Where there are great open plains, watered and fertilised by mighty rivers, we get large populations speaking the great literary languages of India. In the rugged recesses of the mountains we find small communities, divided from one another by physical obstacles which have produced rigid local patriotisms and enmities, and a wonderful variety of savage speeches. The linguist has usually worked independently of the ethnologist, and has come to his own unprejudiced conclusions. It is interesting to find how closely the results of their separate enquiries agree.

Postscript.

Sir H. H. Risley's theory as to the Scythian origin of the Marāthas has not passed unquestioned, and those who wish to see a brief and clear account of the latest theories on the subject should read Mr Crooke's paper on "Rājputs and Marāthas" in Vol. XL. (January—June, 1910) of the *Journal of the Royal Anthropological Institute*. Mr Crooke, who gives copious references to the latest literature on the subject, holds that "the theory that a Hun or Scythian element is to be traced in the population of the Deccan is inconsistent with the facts of tribal history, so far as they can now be ascertained." Mr Crooke thinks that the anthropometrical facts can be explained otherwise than by Saka invasion and an infusion of Scythian blood. "The presence of a brachycephalic strain," he says, "in Southern and Western India need not necessarily imply a Mongoloid invasion from Central Asia. The western coast was always open to the entry of foreign races. Intercourse with the Persian Gulf existed from a very early period, and Mongoloid Akkads or the short-headed races from Baluchistan may have made their way along the coast or by sea into Southern and Western India. But it is more probable that this strain reached India in prehistoric times, and that the present population is the result of the secular intermingling of various race types, rather than of events within the historical period." Mr Crooke's view is supported by the recently issued Census Report of the Bombay Presidency, which says, "the term Marātha is derived by some from two Sanskrit words, *mahā*, 'great,' and *rathi*, 'a warrior.'" According to Sir Rāmkrishna Gopāl Bhandārkar it is derived from Rattas, a tribe which held political supremacy in the Deccan from the remotest time. "The Rattas called themselves Mahā Rattas or Great Rattas, and thus the country in which they lived came to be called Mahārāttha, the Sanskrit of which is Mahā-rāshtra."

Indigenous names are frequently Sanskritised, much as we turn French *chaussée* into "causeway." Sometimes the change is so complete that the original cannot be identified. In some cases the alteration is easily recognised. In Northern Bengal, for instance, is the river *Ti-stā*, a name which belongs to a large group of Tibeto-Burman river names beginning with *Ti-*, or *Di-*, such as *Ti-pai*, *Di-bru*, *Di-kho*, *Di-sāng*, etc., etc. Hindus say the name *Ti-stā* is either a corruption of Sanskrit *Tri-srotas*, "having three streams," or of Tṛṣṇā, "thirst." Etymology and legend, in fact, give but doubtful guidance to the ethnologist, and the best hope of acquiring some real knowledge of Rājput and Marātha origins lies in the possible discovery of coins and inscriptions in the absence of direct historical records.

Chapter II

The Languages of India

It is quite possible to live many years in one province or another of India without obtaining more than the vaguest conception of the linguistic riches of the country. It was Sir G. A. Grierson who rendered it impossible for any but the most careless to ignore the fact that India has not only more languages than Europe, but many more kinds and families of speech. Most Europeans in India live in the populous areas where ethnical and geographical conditions are favourable to the evolution and spread of one of the great literary languages. In Madras, the European comes into contact with one or other of the cultivated Dravidian tongues. In Bombay, he learns that Marāthi and Gujarāti have ancient and interesting literatures. In Calcutta, he is surrounded by millions of Bengalis, who in modern times have as many varieties of literary expression as the most advanced of European races. In Rangoon, he hears the most highly organised of Tibeto-Burman speeches. In Allahabad, Benares, Lahore, Patna, he acquires some smattering of the beautiful and expressive languages which are closest to the model of the original Indo-Aryan idiom. These are the exact counter parts of the great literary languages of Europe, of English, French, German, Italian, etc. But while the European mountains contain one or two shy survivals at most of primitive ways of talking, India has many languages of the type of Basque. In the little frontier province of Assam alone, dozens of grammars and vocabularies have been printed, and much more remains to be done. Happily, an appetite for more information has been aroused by the feast spread before linguists in Sir G. A. Grierson's great *Survey*. He himself is at work on a book which will tell us all that is at present known about the many languages of India, and their relations with one another. But in addition to his own labours, Sir George Grierson has been an apostle of linguistic research and has gathered round him many disciples, not all of whom recognise whence came the impulse that has set them to an examination of the history and growth of Indian languages. Most promising sign of all, native scholars no longer disdain the living tongues of India, nor confine their studies to the classics of Sanskrit, Arabic, and Persian. In Bengal alone, the Proceedings of the *Vangiya Sāhitya Parisat*, a society for the pursuit of linguistic and ethnological research, now form a goodly library of books, and the poet, Rabindranath Tagore, whose own English version of his charming *Gitanjali* is in the hands of all who love poetry or are interested in Indian matters, is also a very keen and competent student of his native language on lines suggested by the enquiries of European scholars. Much has been learnt, but linguistic research in India has still many interesting secrets for the zeal of European students to reveal. In Scandinavia, Germany, France, a new sense of the value of such studies has been aroused. All that can be attempted in the following pages is to show, very summarily and briefly, what is known at present.

We have already seen that there are seven more or less recognisable types of Indian humanity. To these roughly correspond five great families of living vernaculars. The Turko-Iranian, the Indo-Aryan, the Scytho-Dravidian, the Aryo-Dravidian, and the Mongolo-Dravidian races have for the most part acquired Aryan languages which, in their relations to Sanskrit and Persian, may be compared with the Romance languages of Europe in their relations to literary Greek and Latin. The Dravidian races speak one or other of the great Dravidian dialects, or some idiom of the Mundā languages of Chota Nagpore. Among the Mongoloid races of the extreme north and east of India, we find the Mon-Khmer and the Tibeto-Chinese families of speech. Of these, the Dravidian family seems to be confined to India—to the high tablelands of Southern India, with one outlying settlement among the Brāhuis of Baluchistan. This Dravidian speech would seem to be the original and indigenous language of India. The Mundā languages of Chota Nagpore, again, are plainly very ancient Indian tongues and are, in all probability, as aboriginal as the true Dravidian speech. But Mundā tongues have elements in common with the Mon-Khmer languages of Further India, Malacca, and Australonesia. The present explanation of this fact is provided by the supposition that, in prehistoric times, these distant regions shared a common language with great part of Northern India. But, for all practical purposes, the relations of the Mundā languages with the Far East are still so vaguely defined, that they may be provisionally regarded as being as indigenous as their neighbours, the Dravidian languages. The connection of the Mon-Khmer languages with Further India and the Pacific have formed the subject of the now famous researches of Pater Schmidt of Vienna and other German investigators. The Indo-Chinese family of languages is obviously connected with the many dialects of Southern China. An Indian journalist once told me that he thought that the tumbled mountain ranges which separate India from China and form, for the time, a semi-savage "no man's land" of primitive social customs and administration, are the most interesting area on earth. It is an Asiatic and a huger Albania, of whose ethnological and linguistic condition much has yet to be learned. Those who heard Mr Archibald Rose's lectures in London and Cambridge on his travels in these regions will easily realise how much room there is here for anthropological and linguistic research among the rough but attractive races of this quarter.

Lastly, in the great alluvial plain which separates the Himalayas from the tableland of the south, and along the western coast, are the peoples who use one or other of the great Aryan vernaculars, languages of much the same type as the modern languages of Europe, sharing much of their vocabulary, and ultimately derived from similar if still obscure origins. It is of all these languages, and of some of their innumerable dialects (not all of them even now known by name), that some account must be given in this chapter.

PLATE V

Seoris or Savaras
(Mirzapur district)

The history of the languages of India has reflected the long struggle for pre-eminence between the indigenous Dravidian culture of the south and the Aryan civilisation of the north. The Mundā languages are those of an isolated group of highlanders, who, till quite recent times, hardly came into contact with or were influenced by the speech or thought of other races. The Mon-Khmer-speaking people of the Khasi Hills were similarly wholly isolated, and were long supposed to be absolutely aboriginal and separate from other races of men, till quite recent investigations discovered their linguistic affinities with the Mons of Southern Burma and races in French Indo-China. The Tibeto-Burman languages of the north-eastern frontier are the simple and primitive speech of semi-savage men. For such languages, contact with the Aryan languages means rapid decay and dissolution.

Hindu civilisation and Hindu religion find easy converts in the rude and simple Mongoloid people of the north-east, and acceptance of Hindu manners and customs almost always results in a rapid change of language. So again, the Iranian languages represent the final stage in the advance of Islam and its languages as a conquering religion. The Iranian tongues of the north-western frontier are only Indian in the fact that they happen to fall within the administrative border of British India. If we omit all consideration of these races and languages for the present, we shall be free to consider the long struggle between the Aryan and the Dravidian. The Aryan religion, the religion of the Hindus, has spread all over India, and as the Dravidian temples of the south are among the glories of Hindu religious architecture, so the Hinduism of the south is now, in many ways, the most typical and interesting form of the religion. The spread of the Aryan blood has been far less wide in extent, as the previous chapter sufficiently shows. The Aryan languages have spread all over the north of India, up to an irregular line running obliquely across the peninsula from near Vizagapatam on the east coast to near Goa on the west coast. Into the Aryan area projects the rocky plateau of Chota Nagpore, where the Mundā dialects still survive, and there are a few other outlying areas where Dravidian tribes still use the original language of India. With these exceptions, Northern India, from Bombay to Calcutta now speaks Aryan languages.

Let me then begin by giving a brief account of the two ancient and indigenous families of language in India, the Dravidian and Mundā families. Sir G. Grierson's *Survey* has definitely established the fact that, in spite of the close physical resemblance between the Dravidian races properly so called and the inhabitants of Chota Nagpore, there is no linguistic affinity between them. In Sir George Grierson's own words "they differ in their pronunciation, in their modes of indicating gender, in their declensions of nouns, in their method of indicating the relationship of a verb to its objects, in their numeral systems, in their principles of conjugation, in their methods of indicating the negative, and in their vocabularies. The few points in which they agree are points which are common to many languages scattered all over the world."

The Dravidian Languages.

(1) The *Dravidian languages*. These are, as aforesaid, the languages of Southern India. Two of them survive further to the north in Chota Nagpore and the Sonthal Parganas, where they exist side by side with Mundā dialects. One curiously isolated Dravidian language is Brāhui, an extraordinary survival, far to the north-west, in the midst of the Iranian and Muhammadan languages of Baluchistan. The Sanskrit writers knew of two great southern languages which they named the Andhra-bhāshā and the Drāvida-bhāshā. The first corresponded to what is now Telugu and its cognates, the latter to the rest of the southern languages. Sir George Grierson classifies the Dravidian family thus:

	Number of speakers (1901)
A. Drāvida group:	
Tamil	16,525,500
Malayalam	6,029,304
Kanarese	10,365,047
Kodagu	39,191

Tulu	535,210
Toda	805
Kota	1300
Kurukh	592,351
Malto	60,777
B. Intermediate languages:	
Gond, etc.	1,123,974
C. Andhra group:	
Telugu	20,696,872
Kandh	494,099
Kolami	1505
D. Brāhui	48,589
	56,514,524

Sir G. Grierson borrows the following general account of the main characteristics of the Dravidian forms of speech, with slight verbal alterations, from the *Manual of the Administration of the Madras Presidency*:

"In the Dravidian languages all nouns denoting inanimate substances and irrational beings are of the neuter gender. The distinction of male and female appears only in the pronoun of the third person, in adjectives formed by suffixing the pronominal terminations, and in the third person of the verb. In all other cases, the distinction of gender is marked by separate words signifying 'male' and 'female.' Dravidian nouns are inflected, not by means of case terminations, but by means of suffixed postpositions and separable particles. Dravidian neuter nouns are rarely pluralized; Dravidian languages use postpositions instead of prepositions. Dravidian adjectives are incapable of declension. It is characteristic of these languages, in contradistinction to Indo-European, that, wherever practicable, they use as adjectives the relative participles of verbs, in preference to nouns of quality or adjectives properly so called. A peculiarity of the Dravidian (and also of the Mundā) dialects is the existence of two pronouns of the first person plural, one inclusive of the person addressed, the other exclusive. The Dravidian languages have no passive voice, this being expressed by verbs signifying 'to suffer' etc. The Dravidian languages, unlike the Indo-European, prefer the use of continuative participles to conjunctions. The Dravidian verbal system possesses a negative as well as an affirmative voice. It is a marked peculiarity of the Dravidian languages that they make use of relative participial nouns instead of phrases introduced by relative pronouns. These participles are formed from the various participles of the verb by the addition of a formative suffix. Thus 'the person who came' is in Tamil literally 'the who-came'."

It is worth while, for once, to quote this somewhat technical description because it shows that though the Aryan languages have driven the Dravidian languages out of Northern India, the latter may have affected the Aryan speech in the transition which, in common with the corresponding speeches of Europe, it has undergone from inflected to analytic ways of talking.

Tamil. Tamil, or Arava, is spoken all over the south of India and the northern part of Ceylon. It extends as far as Mysore on the west coast and Madras on the east coast. It has been carried all over Further India by emigrant coolies. As might be expected from its geographical position, it is the oldest, richest, and most highly organised of Dravidian languages. It has an extensive literature written in a literary dialect called "Shen" or "perfect" as compared with the colloquial "Kodum" or "rude" speech of ordinary men. The words "Tamil" and "Drāvida" are both corruptions of an original "Drānida." Tamil has an alphabet of its own.

Malayalam. Malayalam is a branch of Tamil which came into existence in the ninth century A.D. It is the language of the Malabar coast, and has one dialect, Yerava, spoken in Coorg. This language has borrowed its vocabulary freely from Sanskrit. It differs from the mother tongue in having dropped the personal terminations of verbs. Its alphabet is the Grantha character, much used in Southern India for writing Sanskrit.

Kanarese. Kanarese is the language of the Kingdom of Mysore and the adjoining British territory. It has an ancient literature written in a character resembling that of Telugu. Its dialects of Badaga and Kurumba are spoken in the Nīlgiri hills. Kodagu, the language of Coorg, is said by some to be a dialect of Kanarese, and is the link between it and Tulu, the language of part of South Kanara in Madras. Toda and Kota will always have an interest for anthropologists in connection with Dr Rivers' now classical investigation into the social life of the Todas.

Gond. The Gond language is spoken outside the true Dravidian area, in the hill country of Central India. It is intermediate between the Drāvida and Andhra languages, and like most hill languages has many dialects. It is unwritten and has no literature.

Telugu. Telugu is the only important Andhra language now surviving. It is the language of the eastern coast from Madras to near the southern border of Orissa. It has an extensive literature written in a character of its own, adapted from the Aryan Devanāgari. This character, like the writing of Orissa, is easily recognised by its loops and curves, said to be due to the difficulty of writing straight lines with a stylus on a palm leaf without splitting the leaf.

Finally there remains the isolated and distant Brāhui language in Baluchistan. Its separate existence has led to a very pretty quarrel between linguists and ethnologists. Dr Haddon in his work on the *Wanderings of Peoples*, in this series, says that "the Dravidians may have been always in India: the significance of the Brāhui of Baluchistan, a small tribe speaking a Dravidian language, is not understood, probably it is merely a case of cultural drift." Sir George Grierson says "if they (the Dravidians) came from the north-west, we must look upon the Brāhuis as the rear-guard; but if from the south, they must be considered as the advance guard of the Dravidian immigration. Under any circumstances it is possible that the Brāhuis alone retain the true Dravidian ethnic type, which has been lost in India proper by admixture with other aboriginal nationalities such as the Mundās." My own diffident suggestion is that the Brāhuis may be a Dravidian race as a survival of emigration when Northern India was also Dravidian, as the French are a "Latin" race.

Of the Mundā languages I need not speak at any length, interesting as they are to students of spoken speech. They are spoken by over three millions of people, and, besides numerous dialects of each, are six in number. They have been carefully studied by missionaries and others, and many of them are now recorded in the Roman character.

I must apologise for a somewhat dull and detailed account of the Dravidian languages. It seemed necessary to explain what manner of languages they were that fought an unequal and not always losing fight with the great Aryan languages of the north. The account of the struggle between the two, on the other hand, has an enduring interest. Dravidian and Aryan languages now face one another much as do French and Breton in Brittany, English and Gaelic in the Highlands, Flemish and French in Belgium. But in the Indian plains the contest was waged on a much vaster scale, and some of the incidents of the long struggle can still be recovered. One point should be carefully borne in mind. In Northern India the Aryan languages and the Hindu religion are openly and completely victorious. The peculiar philosophic and religious ideas of Hinduism find apt and copious expression in the Aryan vocabulary of the north. But Dravidian India, too, in accepting Hinduism, perforce accepted with it much of the Aryan vocabulary. It is Dravidian still, as England is still mainly Germanic. But without Aryan words it could hardly give expression to Hindu speculations and aspirations. As our own language, as these words I write, have a strong intermixture of Latin phrase and idiom, so the Aryan influence has in a greater or less degree penetrated to Ceylon itself, once held by Aryan poets to be the home of demoniac and barbarian races. There are Dravidian traces in the north, survivals of old days of Dravidian supremacy. In the south, a veneer of Aryan culture has been added to the ancient Dravidian civilisation. This was strong to resist a change of idiom: it clung sturdily to most of its vocabulary; but there has been an infusion of Aryan words, needed for ritual and, in some cases, for administrative purposes. The use of the word "administrative" reminds me to say, before passing on, that nowhere in India is English so freely used as in the Dravidian south. Originally Englishmen seem to have found Dravidian languages too difficult a means of communication. But Dravidians themselves soon discovered that English was a convenient *lingua franca*. All India is now making the same discovery, and English is binding the educated classes into a new pan-Indian race.

The Aryan Languages.

We now return to the fascinating story of the spread of the Indo-Aryan languages over the north and west of the peninsula. In the tale, captured from the patient study of words and idioms, and finding only occasional support from legend, and practically none from history, since history had not yet begun to exist, we get a singularly moving and interesting picture of the social existence of vanished tribes of men. We partly know and partly conjecture that there was once a race of men whom we may conveniently call Indo-Europeans who spoke the parent-speech of the modern languages of Europe, Armenia, Persia, and northern India. Probably the Panjāb in very early times was occupied by several immigrations of Indo-European folk, for in the earliest days of which we have any knowledge, the land of the Five Rivers is already the home of many Indo-Aryan tribes, who live at enmity with one another, and have a fraternal habit of speaking of one another as unintelligible barbarians.

In the Sanskrit geography of somewhat later times, India is divided into the sacred Madhya-deça, the "Midland," and the rest. Already this Midland country, the home of the latest immigrants, is considered to be the true habitat of civilised Aryans, all the rest of the peninsula being more or less barbarous. It is important that the reader should understand exactly where this Midland lay. On the north it ended below the foot-slopes of the Himalayas. On the south, it was bordered by the Vindhyā hills, the southern boundary of the Gangetic plain. On the west it extended to Sirhind on the eastern limits of what is now the Panjāb. On the east its limit was the confluence of the Ganges and Jumna. Its inhabitants, of mixed Aryan and Dravidian origin, had spread eastwards from the upper part of the *do-āb*, the watershed between the two rivers. Their language gradually became the current speech of the Midland. It was cultivated as a literary tongue from early times and came to be known as Sanskrit, the "purified" language. Purified and systematised it was by the labours of grammarians and phoneticians, the most famous of whom is Pānini, who lived and wrote about 300 B.C.

To the phonetic acumen of these early grammarians the existing alphabets of northern India, singularly different in arrangement from the confused order of European and Semitic letters, bear testimony. In the Indian alphabets the letters are arranged in order, according to the vocal organs chiefly used in their pronunciation, as Gutturals, Palatals, Cerebrals, Dentals, and Labials. All the phonetic changes which occur in the formation of the numerous compound words are carefully reduced to rule, and the spelling professes to be (what perhaps no spelling ever has been or can be) phonetic.

It is a moot point whether Sanskrit was in Pānini's time a spoken vernacular. It is more probable that it was, what it still remains in most parts of Hindu India, a second and literary language, used much as Latin was used in medieval Europe. The spoken form of the archaic language found in the older Vedas developed into Prākrit, which existed side by side with Sanskrit as the spoken dialects of Italy existed side by side with literary Latin. As the Italian dialects developed into the modern languages of Europe, so the Prākrits gave birth to the Aryan modern languages of India. Thus the latter were not in any accurate sense derived from Sanskrit, but only shared a common origin with it[4]. It remained, however, as a standard of literary perfection and was destined to play an important part in the enrichment of many of the modern languages of India, when contact with western culture brought about what may fairly be called a literary renaissance. This was particularly the case with Bengali. Its medieval literature was all but confined to rhymed hymns and tales. English education led to a revival of Sanskrit studies. From England Bengal learnt that it was possible to write prose in many varied forms, in novels, essays, histories, journalism, and so forth. The medieval literary language, derived from the Prākrit, had grown insufficient for the expression of anything but the simplest devotional or amatory emotion, and Bengali borrowed freely from the rich treasury of Sanskrit.

---

[4] As in Europe, the modern Aryan languages differ from one another chiefly in survivals from the indigenous earlier speech which preceded each of them.

PLATE VI

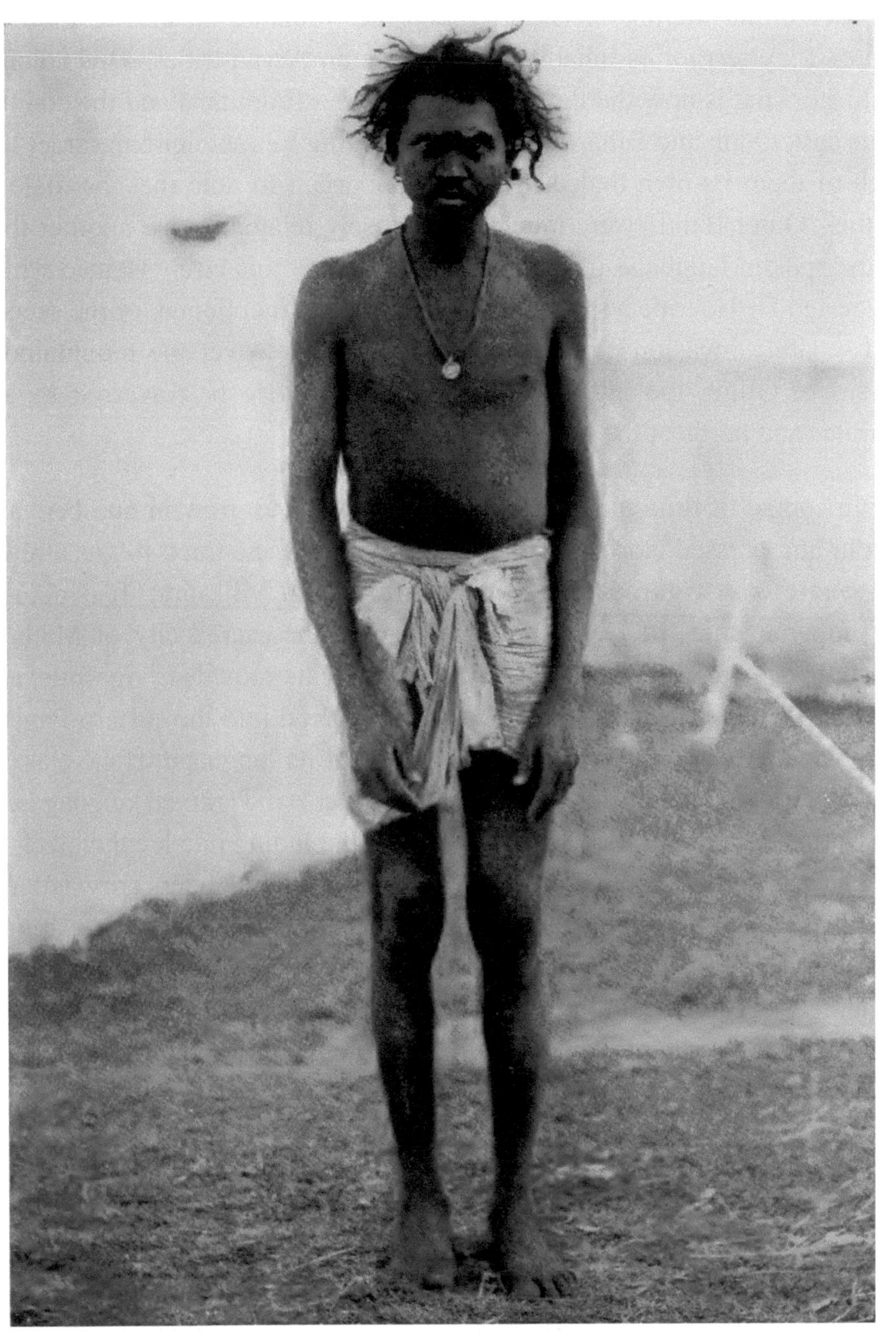

A Bhuiyār
(Mirzapur district)

In the "Midland," then, were various forms of Prākrit, side by side with the sacred and literary Sanskrit. Round the Midland, on the west, south, and east lay territories inhabited by other Indo-Aryan tribes. This country included what is now the Panjāb, Sind, Gujarāt, Rājputānā and the country to its east, Oudh and Bihār. The tribes inhabiting this semicircular tract had each of them its own dialect. But it is important to note that the dialects of this "Outer Band" were much more closely related to one another than to the spoken language of the "Midland." It was this circumstance which suggested Dr Hoernle's ingenious theory, already mentioned, of the second and separate invasion of Aryans into the Midland over the mountainous passes of Gilgit, too high, arduous, and difficult to be traversed by the families and herds of the nomad newcomers.

In course of time the population of the Midland grew in numbers and valour and pressed closely on the food supplies of the tract. It was already the centre of a vigorous and widely influential civilisation. It contained the imperial cities of Delhi and Kanauj, and the sacred city of Mathura (Μόδουρα ἡ τῶν θεῶν, as Ptolemy calls it). This crowded, vigorous, and martial population was bound to expand. It spread into the eastern Panjāb, Rājputānā, Gujarāt and Oudh, carrying with it its language. Hence, as Sir George Grierson points out, we get in this "Outer Band" mixed languages, of the Midland type near the "Midland" centre, but fading into local dialects as we go further west, south, and east. Finally as the Midlanders crowded into the territories of the Outer Band, the inhabitants of these took refuge among the Dravidians of the south and east, and so gave birth to dialects which ultimately became Marāthi in the south and Oriyā, Bengali and Assamese on the east, all of them characteristic languages of the "Outer Band."

I am borrowing so freely and unscrupulously from Sir George Grierson that it is a relief to pause for a moment to interpose a very diffident suggestion of my own. Vocabulary, and even idiom, have become a dubious guide to the constituent elements of the "Outer Band" languages which have almost entirely destroyed the original vocabularies of the Dravidian or Mongolo-Dravidian races who use them. But it is just possible that accentuation, rhythm, metre may furnish some clue to these vanished dialects, which may have bequeathed a characteristic tone of voice to their Aryan successors.

Bengali, for instance, has a very peculiar initial phrasal accent which strongly distinguishes it from the etymologically cognate speech of Bihār, much as the characteristic *accent tonique* of French distinguishes it from Italian and Spanish. Native scholars in Bengal are, I am glad to say, beginning to work at the Dravidian elements in their expressive and copious language, and will, I hope, soon investigate the Mongolian elements, whether of idiom or pronunciation, in the Bengali of the north-eastern part of the province.

To return to Sir George Grierson, he holds that the present linguistic condition of northern India is this:—there is, firstly, a Midland Indo-Aryan language which holds the Gangetic Doāb. Round it on three sides is a band of Mixed languages, in the eastern Panjāb, Gujarāt, Rājputānā and Oudh. With these Sir George includes the Indo-Aryan languages of the Himalayan slopes north of the Midland, which have been introduced in comparatively recent times by immigrants from Rājputānā.

The Prākrits. Before I leave the Aryan languages of India, I must give a brief summary of what Sir George Grierson says of the Prākrits, the spoken speeches which have always, implicitly or explicitly, been distinguished from the artificial and literary Sanskrit. The Primary Prākrits of the Midland and Outer Band (of which latter no record survives) were of the same type as the Latin known to us in literature. They were synthetic and inflected languages. These gradually decayed (or developed) into what Sir G. Grierson calls the Secondary Prākrits. These are still synthetic, but diphthongs and harsh combinations of consonants are avoided, "till in the latest developments we find a condition of almost absolute fluidity, each language becoming an emasculated collection of vowels hanging for support on an occasional consonant." These Secondary Prākrits lasted from the days of the Buddha (550 B.C.) to about 1000 A.D.

One at least of these Secondary Prākrits, Pāli, has obtained world-wide fame as the language of the Buddhist scriptures. Thus crystallised, it underwent the same fate as Sanskrit and became more or less what we call in Europe a "dead" language. In the Midland was a great and famous Prākrit called Sauraseni, after the Sanskrit name, Surasena, of the country round Mathura. In Bihār was Māgadhī; in Oudh and Baghelkhand was Ardhamāgadhī or "half Māgadhī"; south of these was Mahārāshtri, which is best known to students of the ancient Indian drama as the vehicle of the lyrics with which the plays are studded. Kings, sages, heroes and other noble characters speak Sanskrit. Inferior personages use Sauraseni.

The Secondary Prākrits themselves degenerated into what Indian grammarians call Apabhramsas, "corrupt" or "decayed" tongues, which were used for literary purposes and finally became the parents of the great Aryan languages of the present time.

For comparison with the preceding table of the Dravidian languages, I give below the census table of the Aryan languages as recorded in 1901:—

	Number of speakers
A. Language of the Midland:	
Western Hindi	40,714,925
B. Intermediate languages.	
a. More nearly related to the Midland language:	
Rājasthānī	10,917,712
The Pahārī (or 'mountain') languages of the Himalaya	3,124,981
Gujarāti	9,439,925
Panjābi	17,070,961
b. More nearly related to the Outer languages:	
Eastern Hindi	22,136,358
C. Outer languages.	
a. North-western group:	
Kāshmīrī	1,007,957
Kohistānī	36
Lahndā	3,337,917

Sindhī	3,494,971
b. Southern language:	
Marāthī	18,237,899
c. Eastern group:	
Bihārī	34,579,844
Oriyā	9,687,429
Bengali	44,624,048
Assamese	1,350,846

Of all these modern languages, their idioms, their characters, their literature, I do not venture to give even a summarised account. Those who have any curiosity to learn more about them cannot do better than consult Sir George Grierson's work on *The Languages of India*, until it, in its turn, is superseded by the book he is now writing from the materials collected in his *Linguistic Survey*. But everyone who has read *The Newcomes* will want to know what Hindustāni is, especially as it is one of the languages prescribed for the study of probationers for the Indian Civil Service and is taught at the universities of Oxford, Cambridge, London, and Dublin. In the strictest sense Hindustāni is the dialect of western Hindi spoken between Meerut and Delhi. It was much cultivated, as a literary dialect, by both Hindus and Musalmāns. The latter wrote, and write it, in the Persian character, and have added a large number of Persian and Arabic words. In this Persianised form it is known as Urdū, "a name derived from the *Urdū-e mu 'alla*, or royal military bazaar outside the imperial palace at Delhi, where it is supposed to have had its origin." Under Muhammadan rule Urdū was almost as much the *lingua franca* of India as English has come to be in modern times.

Another point is worth noting here. The Aryan languages of northern India are, in a very real sense, Hindu languages. Perhaps I shall make myself clearer by asserting that the languages of Western Europe are Christian languages. For historical reasons, their religious phraseology has a Christian connotation and allusiveness. But in the west, the distinction between things secular and things religious has become so familiar that the Christian element in our speech is not recognisable in our ordinary talk. In Hindu India, on the other hand, almost every act of a man's life has some religious or superstitious significance, and hence all the Aryan languages in the mouths of Hindus are markedly different from the shape they assume when spoken by Musalmāns. In the case of western Hindi we have the recognised Muhammadan dialect of Urdū, but in other languages too there is a Muhammadan dialect or *patois*, even if it has no separate name. A curious exception, however, occurs in eastern Bengal, where the bulk of the population is Musalmān. In this region the Muhammadans are comparatively recent converts from the lower aboriginal or Mongoloid castes, whose Muhammadanism sits very lightly on their habits and consciences, and so far as my own experience goes, there is little difference between the speech of the lower Musalmāns and their friends and cousins the Chandāls and other indigenous castes.

The Indo-Chinese Languages.

Finally, I must say a few words about the Indo-Chinese and Mon-Khmer languages. I spent most of my official life among people speaking these languages, and find, somewhat shamefacedly, that Sir G. A. Grierson makes me responsible for sundry vocabularies compiled in my distant youth. Naturally, I feel a personal interest in the people of the north-eastern border, and am tempted to enlarge on their qualities of speech and character. But I have left myself little space, and the Mongoloid races of the frontier are hardly Indian in any proper sense of the word. Moreover, though their total number is not great, they speak many languages. The Census of 1901 recognises 119 such languages. The most important of them all is, of course, Burmese, which is spoken by about seven and a half millions of people. There are nearly 900,000 Karens in Burma, and about 750,000 Shans. The Meithei (now Manipuris) mentioned above are 272,997 in number. The Boro or Kachari people of the Assam valley, a most attractive and delightful race, number somewhat less than 250,000. The other languages of this type have mostly a much smaller number of speakers than these. But mention should be made of 250,000 Mons, Palungs and Was in Burma, and 177,827

Khāsis in Assam, since these constitute the only members of the Mon-Khmer family still found within the limits of British India.

These people, speaking Indo-Chinese languages, surround India proper on the north and east in a crescent-shaped curve, mostly in the valleys of lofty and rugged mountains. From the eastern mountains projects into the midst of the modern province of Assam a range of hills, dividing the valley of the Brahmaputra from that of Sylhet, which is watered by the Surma. Readers of Sir W. W. Hunter's delightful little book on *The Thackerays in India* will not need to be told where Sylhet is, or what sort of a place it is. This range of hills is inhabited by the Garos on the west, and the Nagas on the east, both Tibeto-Burman races. Between them, on one of the most beautiful plateaus in the world, are the Khāsis, once, as I have said elsewhere, regarded as being as isolated and unique as our European Basques, but now proved to be, linguistically at least, connected with the Mons in Burma, and many races and tribes in Further India and Australonesia.

All these Indo-Chinese people seem to have come originally from north-western China, following the beds of great rivers in their travel; down the Chindwin, the Irrawaddy, and the Salween into Burma, down the Brahmaputra into Assam, and up the Brahmaputra into Tibet. There seem to have been at least three waves of migration. First, in prehistoric times, there was a Mon-Khmer invasion into Further India and Assam. Next, also at an unknown date, was a Tibeto-Burman invasion into the same regions and Tibet. Next the Tai branch of the Siamese-Chinese entered eastern Burma about the sixth century A.D. A fourth Tibeto-Burmese invasion, that of the Kachins, when in Lord Dufferin's time, the British annexed Upper Burma.

I think I have now said enough to show how the languages of India are distributed. It only remains to give a brief and cursory account of the Indian Religions. This is a subject on which big books might be, and have been, written. But, even in so small a book on the Peoples of India it seems necessary to give some account of their religious divisions.

Chapter III

The Religions of India

(1) *Animism.* At the base of all the religions, perhaps at the base of all religions all over the world, lies a mass of primitive beliefs, not perhaps yet consciously classed by the holders of them as distinctly religious, which are called by the question-begging name of Animism. By this statement, I mean merely that many of the more ignorant and simple folk who profess and call themselves Hindus, Buddhists, Jains, Muhammadans, or Christians, are in fact at the animistic stage of intellectual evolution. The religious impulse is there, but has not become specialised. There is no religious theorising, but merely communal and transmitted beliefs about the nature of things in general. Perhaps I had better quote Sir H. H. Risley's definition of Hinduism as it exists in India. "It conceives of man," he says, "as passing through life surrounded by a ghostly company of powers, elements, tendencies, mostly impersonal in their character, shapeless phantasms of which no image can be made and no definite idea can be formed. Some of these have departments or spheres of influence of their own: one presides over cholera, another over small-pox, another over cattle disease; some dwell in rocks, others haunt trees, others, again, are associated with rivers, whirlpools, waterfalls, or strange pools hidden in the depths of the hills. All of them require to be diligently propitiated by reason of the ills which proceed from them, and usually the land of the village provides the means for their propitiation."

If this definition, that of a kindly and experienced student of primitive thought and emotion, be correct, there is already an attempt at analysis and classification. But the analysis is feeble, the classification very elementary. The differences which seem obvious to the civilised man, who inherits the analytic inventions and investigations of long series of ancestors, are not yet realised. There is practically no distinction between things animate and inanimate, since all may be maleficent and must therefore, on occasion, be propitiated. There is no sense of things subter-human, human, and superhuman. Still less, of course, is there any recognition of the difference between things religious and things secular. Grown men face the facts of life as children do, and receive the impressions life conveys to them *en masse*, without making much effort to sort them out. In our own case, we learn to classify from our elders, and classification, literary, scientific, social, religious, is a large part of what we call education. How does primitive man begin to sort out the facts of life, to remember them in classes, to discriminate between human beings and other animals, to place animals above inanimate things, himself above animals, and, finally, the gods above himself? The history of the evolution of Hinduism throws some light on this evolution as it occurred in India.

Meanwhile, it is worth noticing that the Census returns of 1901 returned the Animists of India at only about 8½ millions, or less than 3 per cent. Those who returned themselves as Hindu or Musalmān were so recorded, whatever their degree of mental and social culture. An attempt has been made in the Census of 1911 to distinguish between true Hindus and Animists who call themselves Hindu. How far the attempt was successful, I do not know. I can well believe that it was not welcomed even by educated and intelligent Hindus. Many years ago, I remember a highly educated Hindu in Bengal telling me that there is no distinction between Animists and Hindus; that an Animist is merely a Hindu "in the making" as it were. But perhaps that assertion only amounted to an admission that the Hindu mind is averse from the kind of intellectual evolution by conscious analysis and classification which is dear to Western imaginations. Yet the history of Hinduism and its branches shows that such an evolution has taken place.

PLATE VII

A Ghāsiya
(Mirzapur district)

I should like to suggest that at the stage of human evolution which we call animistic, man takes the facts of life in the lump, as it were, and does not sort them out into classes. If we are to judge by what we know of the history of Hinduism, the evolution of primitive man from this unclassifying stage is something as follows. Art comes into play. The practice of song and draughtsmanship introduces specialisation. From singing comes verse, from drawing comes some kind of rude writing. The first trains the memory, the second aids memory. Then comes the social classification which results from the breaking up of clans, and contact with other clans and communities. All men are not the same, and the difference is grasped and finds expression in language. The new power of classification is extended to other things. The difference between animate and inanimate things is understood, and their relative powers of helping or hurting the tribal community. When classification has proceeded thus far, the inference is easy that as what is known of the faculties of subter-human beings and things to benefit or hurt humans does not by any means account for the joys and calamities of life, there must be a class of superhuman beings who are to be conciliated. By their supposed deeds they are judged. If they are, on the whole, kindly and easily placated, they will be classified by some title which they will usually share with great and good men. If their action on mankind be harmful, they will bear the names given to malicious or inimical races or individuals. At a subsequent stage of analytical evolution their generic names will be confined to their own class; they will be gods or demons. Many Hindus have hardly gone beyond this stage, and we can hardly be surprised that some objection should be taken to too rigid a distinction between Hindus and Animists. In practice, it is often difficult to say whether a given observance is Animistic or Hindu. Here is one case, out of thousands that occur in India, from my own experience. In the seaport town of Chittagong is the shrine of the famous Muhammadan saint Pir Badr, a holy man often invoked by travellers on sea or river. In a niche in a little pillar in the open air, Christians and Buddhists, Hindus and Musalmāns alike place lighted candles by way of propitiation. This, surely, is an observance of the Animistic type. It has no part in any theorised or classified religious system. It is merely the attempt to gratify an influence which may help or harm. Animism is consistent with the most vivid, if childlike, curiosity. All is grist that comes to that primitive mill. But the resulting flour of thought is, as it were, coarse and unsifted.

Artistic specialisation, the birth of literature, brings a need of classification. Out of propitiation comes ritual, a belief in the efficacy of sacramental gestures, offerings, formulæ. But, as time goes on, they are appropriated to the service of highly specialised deities. As man learns the advantage of a division of labour and a specialisation of function, so his gods become "departmental." The classification will not be that of modern times. Among animate things will be reckoned fire, and air, the sun and moon and the twinkling stars. But the process of analysing and sorting will have begun.

(2) *The Vedas.* The Aryan immigrants seem to have brought a scanty and summary theology with them, or it may be that in different surroundings they forgot their old religious ideas, and, with the help of Dravidian and other aboriginal speculations, evolved new ones. Sir G. Grierson has suggested that the fact that they migrated in two afterwards hostile bodies finds its reflection, in the Vedas, in the fabled antagonism of the rival priests Visvāmitra and Vasishta; in the Mahābhāratā in the famous war between the Kauravas and Pāndavas, the Eastern counterpart of the siege of Troy.

The Vedas are four collections of ritual hymns, used in connection with the oblation of the intoxicating juice of the Soma, the moon-plant, or with the sacrificial Fire. The Rig-veda (the oldest) and its supplement the Sāma-veda are now held to have been composed when the Aryans had reached the junction of the Panjāb rivers with the Indus: the Black and White Yajur-veda when they reached the Sutlej and the Jumna; the Atharva-veda, which contains the lower beliefs of aboriginal races, when they had reached Benares. There are gods and goddesses of the sky, the most important being the Sun, and Varuna (the Greek οὐρανός), afterwards a kind of Hindu Neptune, but in these early days represented as sitting in the vault of heaven, and having the sun and stars as the eyes with which he watches the doings of men. His function was to encourage personal holiness as a human ideal. In the mid-air Indra became pre-eminent on Indian soil, where the dependence of an agricultural people on periodical rains made the rain-god an important deity. On earth the most important deities are Soma and Agni (fire) already mentioned. There was also Yama, the beautiful and stately god of death, who though naturally immortal chose to die, and lead the way for mortal successors to the abodes of the dead. Besides the departmental gods, there is in the Vedas a distinct foreshadowing of Pantheism.

(3) *The Brāhmanas.* When the Aryans reached the "Midland," the upper Gangetic valley, the Vedic hymns were supplemented by new Scriptures, called Brāhmanas, which were digests of dicta on matters of ritual for the guidance of priests. These were the beginning of Brāhmanism. The elementary Pantheistic theory of the Vedas was developed into a belief in one Spiritual Being or Ātman. When manifested and impersonal, this Being was the neuter Brahma; when regarded as the Creator, he was the masculine Brahmā; but when manifested in the highest order of intellectual men, he was Brāhman, the Brāhman priestly class. Following the Brāhmanas, was a third order of religious literature, the Upanishads. Dr Hopkins has thus summarised the teaching of these three Scriptures. "In the Vedic hymns, man fears the gods. In the Brāhmanas man subdues the gods, and fears God. In the Upanishads man ignores the gods and becomes God." Not that these three kinds of Scripture, these three evolutions of religious speculation, followed one another in chronological order. But this was, roughly, the logical evolution. Finally the doctrine was established that knowledge leads to the supreme bliss of absorption into Brahmā, and with this was combined the theory of transmigration.

Even from this extremely crude and simplified statement, it will be evident that the priesthood had secured for themselves an unexampled supremacy, and, in the Midland at least, had placed the administrator and warrior in a state of marked inferiority. But in the surrounding territories, success in arms and government won men the consideration still considered their due among ourselves. In the Midland itself the territory was divided among a number of petty chiefs, who waged perpetual warfare with one another. They were not likely to ignore the prestige won by valour and warlike skill. One of them was Gautama, the Buddha (*c.* 596-508 B.C.). Another was Vardhamāna, his contemporary, the founder of Jainism. This is not the place to tell of Buddhism, which, as a recognised creed, though it has spread far to the north and east, and is the religion of Ceylon and Burma, only survives in India proper in faint influences on the belief and practice of various Hindu sects.

(4) *Jainism.* The Jain Reform still exists and numbers over a million of followers. Its doctrines have a vague and general resemblance to those of Buddhism, not because either copied the other, but because they sprang from a common origin. In both Nirvāna, the "blowing out," as it were, of the lamp of life is the goal aimed at. But to the Buddhist, Nirvāna means the peace of extinction; to the Jain, it is final escape from the body after various metamorphoses. Mr Crooke defines the fivefold vow of the Jains as prescribing (1) the sanctity of human life; (2) renunciation of lying, which proceeds from anger, greed, fear or mirth; (3) refusal to take things not given; (4) chastity; (5) renunciation of worldly attachments. The Jain pantheon consists of deified saints who are either Tīrthan-kara, "making a passage through the circuit of life," or Jina, "the victorious ones."

(5) *Hinduism Proper.* These reforms, joined with the spread of the Brāhmanical faith into lands where the authority of Aryan priests was not recognised, produced something which, in its way, resembles the Protestant Reformation. The Vedic religion had come to be the monopoly of a limited order of hereditary priests. This ritual supremacy was broken up by two influences. A new national ideal of worship found expression in the Epics, which to this day, in metrical translations, are the layman's scripture all over India. Secondly, the Vedic pantheon was enormously enlarged by the admission of non-Aryan deities and aboriginal modes of worship. Hence arose the body of writings known as the Purānas, or "ancient" books, not all really old in the trace of their composition, but perhaps deserving their title as containing very old beliefs. Of all these books and their teaching other authorities have written recently in various works on the early history and religious poetry of India, and it would therefore be presumptuous for me to say anything about the religious literature of Hinduism. It is sufficient to say that the Epics introduced, in place of the vague and shadowy Vedic gods, heroic incarnations of divine virtue, wisdom and valour, and thus led to the sectarian worship of the two active members of a new supreme triad of gods, Brahmā, the creator, Vishnu, the preserver, and Siva, the destroyer. Most Hindus are now followers of one or other of the two latter in some incarnation. In early times this sectarian rivalry led to wars and persecutions, but Hinduism is singularly tolerant in matters of belief and doctrine. A Saiva is not a disbeliever in the divinity of the incarnations of Vishnu; a Vaishnava

recognises the ascetic powers of Siva. But each has his favourite deity and chiefly studies the scriptures relating to him. The principal incarnations of Vishnu are Krishna and Rāma, who seem to have been originally deified heroes of the Midland. There were many Vishnuvite reformers, some of whom, it is interesting to note, may have derived suggestions from the early Christianity of Southern India.

The first of these was Rāmānuja, who lived in the eleventh century A.D. Fifth in succession to him was Rāmānanda, who lived in the fourteenth century and was the missionary of popular Vaishnavism in Northern India. To him that tract owes the prevalence of the cult of Rāma and his wife Sītā, the hero and heroine of the Epic known as the Rāmāyana. His chief innovation was the admission of low-caste disciples into the communion. His disciple, the famous Kabir (1380-1420 A.D.), went further. He even linked Hinduism with Islam. Himself a humble weaver, he taught the spiritual equality of all men. God is one, he argued, by whatever name men choose to call Him. The accidents of life, social station and caste, happiness and grief, prosperity and misfortune, are all the results of Māya or Illusion. Happiness comes not by formula or sacrifice but by passionate adoration (*bhakti*) of God. Kabir's chief importance in the history of Hindu evolution is in the fact that his doctrines were the origin of Sikhism.

Another great name in the democratic Vaishnava reformation was that of Chaitanya (1485-1527 A.D.). Mr E. A. Gait writes of him that he was "a Baidik Brāhman. He preached mainly in Central Bengal and Orissa, and his doctrine found ready acceptance among large numbers of the people, especially among those who were still, or had only recently ceased to be, Buddhists. This was mainly due to the fact that he drew his followers from all sources, so much so that even Muhammadans followed him. He preached vehemently against the immolation of animals in sacrifice, and the use of animal food and stimulants, and taught that the true road to salvation lay in bhakti, or fervent devotion to God. He recommended Rādhā worship, and taught that the love felt by her for Krishna was the highest form of devotion. The acceptable offerings were flowers, money, and the like; but the great form of worship was the Sankirtan, or procession of worshippers playing and singing. The peculiarity of Chaitanya's cult is that the post of spiritual guide, or Goshain, is not confined to Brāhmans, and several of those best known belong to the Baidya caste[5]."

The Sikhs. As a religious system, the creed of the Sikhs originated from the Hindu teaching of Kabir, and may yet be reabsorbed into Hinduism, though the Census of 1911 shows that it still flourishes as a separate religion. It began as a religious reform and ended by being a political organisation. It was founded by the Guru Nānak (1469-1538 A.D.) in the Panjāb. Its formula was the Unity of God and the Brotherhood of Man. Ultimately it became a martial brotherhood, one of whose objects was by training, diet, and self-denial to present a strong front to the encroachments of Muhammadan invaders from across the north-west frontier. Circumstances led the Sikh confederacy to try its fortune in arms in two fiercely fought campaigns with the growing power of our East India Company. Defeat was followed by a loyal acceptance of British supremacy, and the Sikhs rival the Gurkhas as the best soldiers in the Indian army. Their services during the mutiny of 1857 will never be forgotten.

The Sāktas. One other great Hindu sect, that of the Sāktas, must be briefly mentioned. It worships the active female principle (*prakriti*) of one or other of the forms of the Consort of Siva—Durgā, Kāli, or Pārvati. This cult arose in Eastern Bengal or Assam about the fifth century, A.D., and has its own scriptures in the Tantras. This sect is probably due to the recrudescence of very ancient aboriginal cults. It is associated with blood-offerings and libidinous rites. It was denounced by the Vaishnava reformers, but still survives, even among educated men. It affected the later forms of Buddhism.

Finally, by omitting all mention of numerous modern Vaishnava sects, we come to the modern Theistic sects. The Brahmo Samāj of Bengal was founded by the celebrated Raja Ram Mohan Roy (1774-1833) who died and was buried at Clifton. His teachings were continued and developed by his successors Maharshi Devendranāth Tagore (the father of the poet Rabindranāth Tagore), Keshav Chandra Sen, and Pratāp Chandra Majumdār.

---

[5] Some account of the development of Chaitanya's teaching in Assam may be found in an article of mine in Dr Hastings' *Dictionary of Religion and Ethics*.

All of these were men of much piety, eloquence, and learning. Sir Alfred Lyall says that "Brahmoism, as propagated by its latest expounders, seems to be unitarianism of a European type, and as far as one can understand its argument, appears to have no logical stability or *locus standi* between revelation and pure rationalism; it propounds either too much or too little to its hearers." It has, however, been an effectual bar to the spread of Christianity among the educated classes in Bengal. It enables them to remain in touch with Hinduism, from which an adoption of any European creed would effectually divide them. Its services of praise and prayer, with a sermon or discourse, are held on Sundays, and in form resemble those of the Christian free churches. Its creed consists in a belief in the Unity of God, the brotherhood of man, and direct communion with God without the intervention of any mediator. It may fairly be claimed for it that it has satisfied the religious needs of men most of whom lead exemplary and in some cases saintly lives, without compelling them to join what is regarded as a foreign and uncongenial religion. But for Ram Mohan Roy, educated Bengal might well have furnished the nucleus of a Christian Church of India, since, before his time, many distinguished and able converts were made. I need only mention the late Rev. K. M. Bannerjee. The Brahmo Samāj is divided into three sections. The Ādi Samāj, as its name indicates, is the original church. It is the most conservative of the three, and takes its inspiration wholly from the Hindu scriptures, and especially from the Upanishads. The Navavidhān Samāj, founded by Keshav Chandra Sen, "the Church of the New Dispensation," is much more eclectic and has borrowed what it considers acceptable, not only from the holy books of Hinduism, but from Christianity, Buddhism, and Islam. The Sādhāran (or "general") Brāhmo Samāj is the most advanced of the three Churches. It rejects caste and the seclusion of women, allows inter-caste marriages, and is seemingly as far from orthodox Hinduism as from orthodox Christianity. It has even allowed one of its lady members to be married to an Englishman by Brāhmo rites. If it can hardly be called Hindu in ritual or in belief, it is Hindu in what is probably regarded as the more important sense of being a purely Indian sect and not a direct product of European missionary zeal.

Another new sect, the Ārya Samāj, or Aryan Society, has much influence in the Panjāb and North-Western India generally. It was founded by Dayānand Saraswati (1827-53). Its only scriptures are the Vedas. It professes pure monotheism, repudiates idol worship, and is much interested in social reform. It has also at times been mixed up, more or less directly, with political agitation. Like the Brāhmo Samāj, it is probably due in its inception to the influence of European religious teaching, but, as is perhaps natural, its acceptance of European ethics is marked by a sturdy resistance to European dogma.

The great bulk of Hinduism, however, remains still but little removed from the Animistic stage of religious evolution, and one of the results of the spread of British rule into wild and savage tracts has been the extension of the borders of Hinduism in competition with Christianity. In the rougher and wilder races, not yet sufficiently softened and civilised for the acceptance of the Hindu social system, the Christian missionary prevails. He has been most successful among the Gonds of Central India, among such savage tribes as the Nāgas, Gāros, and Lushais on the Assam border. Elsewhere Hinduism pursues its quietly imperturbable course and admits savage races to its lower castes as it has always admitted them during the last two thousand years.

Islam in India. Since King George V has more Muhammadan subjects than any other ruler on earth—some 75,000,000 in number, it would not be proper to close a little book on the Peoples of India without saying something of those of their number who are Musalmāns. The early Muhammadan invasions of the tenth century were mere predatory raids, and were attended neither by settlement nor conversion. But at the end of the twelfth century Muhammad Ghori overthrew the Hindu dynasties of Delhi and Kanauj and thus opened the way to future Muhammadan conquests. In the sixteenth century Moghal rule was established under Babar and his successors. During the preceding five centuries Hindu India suffered much oppression and wrong at the hands of Muhammadan invaders, but Islam had made no attempt to become an Indian religion. The early Moghal emperors were too busy in consolidating their conquests and organising their administration to have much leisure or inclination for proselytising. Their policy depended largely on co-operation with Rājput princes, whose daughters they married. The influence of Rājput empresses and princesses made for kindly tolerance. It was only under the zealot Aurangzeb that any tendency to forcible conversion showed itself.

The final result of some seven hundred years of Muhammadan rule in various parts of the country is that Musalmāns are in excess of Hindus only in the Western Panjāb, which is in contact with a purely Muhammadan country, and in Eastern Bengal, where the aboriginal low-caste Hindu was glad to get social promotion by accepting Islam, and where he thrives and prospers at the expense of his Hindu brother, partly because his diet is more nutritious, partly because he does not practise infant-marriage and other debilitating customs.

As has been said above, Animism has affected Islam as well as Hinduism. From the old religion of the country Musalmāns have borrowed demonology, a belief in witchcraft, and the worship of departed Pirs or saints. The most remarkable instance of the latter is the sect of the Pachpiriyas of Bengal, the worshippers of the Five Saints, a cult which some have traced to the cult of the five Pāndava heroes of the Mahābhārata. The five Pirs, however, vary in name from district to district. In Eastern Bengal, no one, whether Hindu or Musalmān (or, I had almost said, Christian), begins a journey by boat without a loud and hearty invocation of the Ganges, the Wind, the Five Pirs, and Pir Badr before mentioned.

Of the two great sects of Islam, the Sunnis and the Shias, the former are by far the most numerous in India. The Sunnis or Traditionalists accept the Sunnat or collected body of Arabic usage as possessing authority concurrent with that of the Koran, which is the sole scripture of the Shias. Yet in Eastern Bengal the annual procession of the Tazias, or representations of the tombs of the martyred grandsons of the Prophet, is much attended by Sunnis (though for them the practice is unorthodox), and indeed by Hindus also. In other parts of India, the Mohurram festival has often led to serious encounters between Hindus and Musalmāns, and even in Calcutta and Bombay has been the cause of dangerous riots.

The sects of Islam in India, unlike the Hindu sects, are not due to the instinct for differentiation, for obvious reasons. They are, in Mr Crooke's words, either puritanical or pietistic. Consequently, followers of them are apt to show a tendency to fanaticism. The Hindu sectarian adores some favourite deity, but does not deny the merits, or the Hinduism, of other deities or their followers. The Musalmān sectarian is one who has discovered a higher orthodoxy than others, or a straighter road to religion, and regards those who do not share his views as an enemy of God and the true faith. Of the puritanical sects, the best known is that of the Wahābis, founded by Ibn Abdul Wahāb at Nejd in Arabia, at the beginning of the eighteenth century. It was an attempt to revive primitive Muhammadanship without the corruptions and accretions of later ages and foreign lands. It was brought into India by Sayid Ahmad Shāh, who proclaimed a Jihād, or holy war, against the Sikhs in 1826. The Wahābis hold that the doctrine of the Unity of God has been endangered by the excessive reverence paid to the Prophet, to his successors the Imāns, and to shrines. At times Wahābis have given trouble to the administration, especially in Bengal. In recent years, however, they call themselves Ahl-i-hadīs, or "followers of tradition," and employ themselves chiefly in endeavouring to eradicate modern superstitions.

The pietistic sects tend towards Sūfi-ism, a combination of Aryan pantheism with Semitic monotheism, which takes the form of ecstatic devotion. Something of the same kind may be found in the Vaisnav sects of Hinduism, and in both cases ultimate absorption in the divinity is the goal aimed at.

Very interesting local communities of Muhammadans are the Moplahs of the Malabar coast, descendants of Arab settlers; the Bohras or "traders" of Western India; and the Khojās, followers of the "Old Man of the Mountain," whose present representative is H.H. the Agha Khān of Bombay, who has many friends in England.

The Pārsīs. The word Pārsī simply means Persian, and the Pārsī religion is the dualistic faith, combined with fire-worship, of the ancient Persians. It is also called Mazdaism from Ahura Mazda (Ormuzd), who is in perpetual conflict with Angro Mainyush (Ahriman), the spirit of evil. It is also called Zoroastrianism, from the reformer Zoroaster, the Greek form of the old Iranian Zarathushtra, the modern Persian Zardusht. The religious phraseology of the Pārsīs shows that their faith must have had a common origin with the Aryan religion of India before the Iranian and Indo-Aryan migrations parted company. By a curious trick of language, the Devas, who in India and Europe are beneficent gods, in Persia become evil spirits. In India by a corresponding inversion, the word Asura, which in the Rig-veda is still a name of gods, was applied to hostile (generally aboriginal) demons. By a further process Asura was regarded as a negative word, and gave birth to a tribe of beneficent Suras. In the earlier times, there were both Ahura and Daeva worshippers, the former being socially superior, cattle-breeders, who, like the Indian Hindus, venerated the cow. It was Zoroaster's mission to fuse these two cults into a dualistic creed, whose main principle was the continuous struggle between the powers of good and evil. Submerged for a time during the Greek occupation, the Mazdaist faith revived under the Sassanids, but was finally overthrown by the advent of Islam, which persecuted and strove to extirpate the worship of fire.

Many of the survivors migrated to India, where they secured the tolerance of Hindu and Muhammadan rulers alike, and increased and multiplied. Up to the middle of the eighteenth century, Surat, Nausāri, and the neighbouring parts of Gujarāt were their home. When, under British rule, Bombay became a great commercial port, large numbers of Pārsīs migrated thither, and in many cases won great wealth and influence.

In the early days of their dispersion, the weak colonies of Pārsīs assimilated themselves with the lower classes of Hindus by whom they were surrounded. But fresh accessions from Irān, and a growth of national prosperity and self-confidence brought about a restoration of the ancient faith. On Indian soil, the Pārsīs now number 94,000. But owing to their intelligence and wealth, due to their remarkable success in trading, the Pārsīs command a much wider political and social influence than their numbers would seem to show. According to Pārsī belief, the soul passes after death to paradise (Bihisht) or a place of punishment (Dozakh) according to a man's conduct in life. Much importance is attached to the performance of rites to the *manes* of ancestors. Fire, water, the sun, moon, and stars were created by Ahura Mazda, and are venerated, as is Zarathushtra the Prophet. Soshios, his son, will some day be reincarnated as a Messiah, and will convert the world to the true faith. As with other Indian religions, contact with Europeans tends to produce laxity of belief and conduct.

Christianity. It is interesting to remember that there were Christians in India before the Christian faith reached our islands. The tradition that St Thomas was the Apostle of India, and suffered martyrdom there, is indeed discredited. This tradition originated with the Syriac *Acta Thomae*, and was accepted by Catholic teachers from the middle of the fourth century. The Indian King Gundaphar of the *Acta* is undoubtedly the historical Gondophares, whose dynasty was Parthian, though his territories were loosely considered to extend to India. A full account of the traditions connecting St Thomas with India (by W. R. Philipps) will be found in vol. XXXII. of the *Indian Antiquary*, 1903, pp. 1-15, 145-160.

The term "Christians of St Thomas" is often applied to the members of the ancient Christian churches of Southern India which claim him as their first founder, and honour as their second founder a bishop called Thomas, who is said to have come from Jerusalem to Malabar in 345 A.D. According to local tradition, St Thomas went from Malabar to Mylapur, now a suburb of Madras and the seat of a Roman Catholic bishop. Here still exists the shrine of his martyrdom on Mount St Thomas. A miraculous cross is shown with a Pahlavi inscription which is said to be as old as the end of the seventh century. The old churches of the south were certainly of East Syrian origin. They never wholly lost their sense of connection with their mother church, for it is known that they sent deputies in 1490 to the Nestorian patriarch Simeon, who provided them with bishops. Under Musalmān rule, they suffered severely, and welcomed the advent of the Portuguese to India. They were, however, recalcitrant to Roman influence, and it was with much difficulty that in 1599 they were induced to submit to a formal union with Rome at the synod of Diamper (Udayamperur in Cochin). During the following century and a half the Thomasine churches were under foreign Jesuit rule, but yielded an unwilling and intermittent obedience. In 1653, there was a great schism, and of about 200,000 Christians of St Thomas only 400 remained loyal to Rome, though some of their churches were soon won back by the Carmelites. The remainder fell under the influence of the Jacobite Mar Gregorius, styled patriarch of Jerusalem, who reached

Malabar in 1665 as an emissary from Ignatius patriarch of Antioch. From this time, the independent churches of Southern India have been Jacobite. At the present time, they are on friendly terms with the Anglican church in India, and are loosening their dependence on the Jacobite patriarch of Antioch.

Of missionary work in India I need not speak in a book of this size. There are nearly three millions of Christians in India, of whom two and a half millions are native converts. Seeing that missionary work has been in operation since 1500, a tale of converts amounting to less than one per cent. may seem a discouraging result of over 400 years of contact with European religious thought. But actual conversion has taken place chiefly among the lower classes and least advanced races. Among the educated classes the influence of Christianity has been indirect, and in many cases has produced a transformation in ethical belief and social conduct as complete as could have been wrought by open conversion. The Brāhmo Samāj, for instance, remains Hindu in a sense, because it refuses to sever its connection with India, or to acknowledge European authority in matters of religion. But the Brāhmo Samāj could not have come into existence but for Rām Mohan Roy's friendly and intimate acquaintance with European Christians and Unitarians. Even in the matter of conversion, the rate of progress is increasing rapidly, partly because missionary effort is being directed to savage tracts hitherto unvisited by civilised men, but partly, also, because the native Christian community is beginning to have sufficient self-confidence and status to proselytise in its turn. The multiplicity of missionary agencies, due to the accidents of European history and development, has been an impediment. Such terms as the Church of England, Church of Scotland, Welsh Baptists, American Baptists, etc., can have little signification for races who cannot be expected to know the historical causes which brought about these local varieties of Christian doctrine and practice. There may yet arise among one of the rival churches in India a Christian Rāmanuja or Chaitanya, who may found a great Church of India, with a ritual, and, perhaps, doctrines of its own. The most successful of the Jesuit missionaries, Robert de Nobili[6] for instance, and such men as the Abbé Dubois in later times, owed their

[6] In 1606, R. de Nobili, a nephew of Bellarmine, was in charge of the Jesuit mission at Madura, and adopted the costume of a Dravidian Brāhman.

success to the fact that they assumed the habits, dress, and often the titles of Brāhmanic ascetics. They could not assume the dusky skin which, after all, is the first and easiest means of gaining an Indian's confidence. They could not wholly accept caste, they could not wink at polygamy in the case of men whose first wives were infertile, and who had an hereditary sense that the lack of an heir is socially and religiously reprehensible. Perhaps a truly indigenous Church of India may deal with such difficulties more successfully than men who are compelled to teach, not only the elements of the Christian faith, but the ethical traditions belonging to their own race.

In this connection, I may be allowed to conclude my necessarily brief story of Indian races and religions with an anecdote. Just thirty-five years ago I was in charge of a "subdivision" in Bengal which contained a large number of native Christians belonging to the Church of England. There were several churches with parsonages, and the nearest of these to my headquarters was in the charge of a young missionary who was glad to have an occasional chat with a young magistrate. One day my missionary friend told me that he had discovered with dismay that his flock were in the habit of attending the Communion Service in batches, according to their castes, so as not to be obliged to drink out of the cup with men of alien caste. There were Hindu Christians and Muhammadan Christians who could not eat or drink together. He decided that this state of things must be stopped at all costs, as being wholly contrary to Christian teaching. I ventured to suggest that spiritual equality is not the same thing as social equality, but had to admit that caste is not usually recognised as a Christian institution. Apparently the Christians listened to their pastor's admonition, for, a few days after, he rode over to say that, in consequence of ex-scavengers and ex-Brāhmans having communicated together, his whole congregation had been put out of caste by their Hindu neighbours. This may not, at first sight, seem a very serious calamity. But it happened that, in the caste specialisation which had survived among the Christians, there were none of the community who were barbers or midwives by caste. Christian men were going about with stubbly chins: worse still, Christian women were in need of help which their Hindu sisters refused to supply. It was a difficult situation for two young bachelors. However, I now confess, after all these years, that I brought a little official pressure to bear on the midwives, and the situation was saved for the moment.

In those days, the educational policy of Government was to give grants-in-aid to primary schools, most of which, in this very Christian "subdivision" were either Roman Catholic or Anglican. When next I proceeded to issue my doles according to school-population and other educational results, I was astonished to find that the Roman Catholic grant-in-aid had increased greatly and the Anglican grant-in-aid had proportionally diminished. This was the immediate (and no doubt temporary) result of my missionary friend's zeal. Such survivals of old beliefs are common in all the religions of India. The main social impulse of the people was implanted on their minds at the distant epoch of the Aryan settlement, the sense of social and racial inequality which has now hardened into the caste system. To most Indians a recognition of the importance and value of caste is the first step towards decent and seemly conduct, towards civilised morality. When a semi-savage hill-man begins to recognise his inferiority to his Hindu neighbours and makes tentative approaches with a view to inclusion in civilised society, his first duty is to abjure the diet of pork and rice-beer which his unregenerate appetite loves, since these indulgences stand in the way of sharing a meal with Hindu folk. (In other parts of India, liquor and meat are consumed by low-caste Hindus of aboriginal origin.) In Assam, a Kachāri first accepts the *sarana* or "protection" of a Hindu Goshain. He is then called a Saraniya Koch. His next step is to abandon strong drinks, on which he is promoted to the status of a Modāhi Koch. At this stage, he may be fortunate enough to win the hand of a bride of pure Koch family, and, under her guidance, acquires enough of conventional habits and beliefs to be recognised as a Kāmtāli or Bor Koch, and is a true Hindu, a member of a genuine Hindu caste. Musalmāns and Christians have other social conventions, and do not usually regard them as essential to good manners or godliness. But their converts retain their social superstitions and carry them into the new surroundings, where they sometimes come into disagreeable contact with the ethical ideas belonging to imported religions.

The contact of Aryan with Dravidian races, some three thousand years ago, brought about the beginnings of caste, which, from one point of view, may be regarded as a rude form of "race-protection," a primitive system of eugenics. It is still most rigidly enforced in the south, where the semi-Aryan classes are in a great minority. It is most relaxed in the Panjāb, where, though caste rules exist, the population is, and probably always has been, as homogeneous as our own race. French travellers in India have sometimes said, half-humorously, that the Anglo-Indian administrators and merchants are practically a caste unto themselves. Bengalis have made the same remark and have said that our Civil Service is composed of *Kali Yuger Brāhman*, "the Brāhmans of the Iron Age." There was once some truth in the accusation, if accusation it be. It was not our business to interfere deliberately with caste, since British policy from the first has been one of kindly neutrality and toleration. Whether indirect influences have mitigated the effect of the sentiment of caste is a moot point. Educated Indians who have lived in Europe see its irksomeness, and in some cases denounce it more vigorously than most Europeans will care to denounce a system due to historical causes which are still partly operative. On the other hand, railways and other facilities for travel, though they have necessarily introduced laxity in matters of food and contact, have probably heightened the caste feeling by emphasising the variety of Hindu humanity and of the customs and habits of its many races. Hence the evolution of Indian society remains as interesting and as incalculable as ever.

In a little book of this sort it has been necessary to make many general and sweeping statements which are not always literally true of any given part of India. But perhaps enough has been said to show the interesting and significant differences between the three hundred odd millions of Western Europe and the three hundred odd millions of India. Our business in India has been primarily to keep the peace, to provide a breathing-space after the social and political turmoil that followed on the breaking-up of the Moghal empire. The principal result, so far, has been a notable increase in Hindu self-confidence and ambition, and a growing belief among Hindus that their ancient social system is not incompatible with industrial, commercial, and political advance on European lines. This belief has been much strengthened by the modernisation of Japan, and its results. It has been fostered by the free admission of educated Hindus to the highest and most responsible posts in the King-Emperor's administration. Inasmuch as that statement brings me to the most modern development of Hindu life and thought, I cannot do better than end at this point.

Bibliography

Chapter I

The standard authority on the Hindu literary theory of Caste is M. Emile Senart's *Les Castes dans l'Inde*. Paris. Ernest Leroux. 1896.

Probably the best succinct account of Caste is Mr E. A. Gait's article in Dr Hastings' *Encyclopædia of Religion and Ethics*. This will, of course, be brought up to date in the forthcoming Report on the Indian Census of 1911.

Sir A. C. Lyall's *Asiatic Studies*. London. John Murray. Contains a sympathetic and learned account of Hindu social life and of the workings of Caste in Upper India.

M. C. Bouglé's *Essai sur le Régime des Castes*. Paris. Felix Alcan. 1908. Contains much interesting matter taken from many sources, but sometimes, from want of local knowledge, does not sufficiently discriminate between different developments of the caste system.

There is an enormous literature on the races, tribes, and castes of India, but references to the most important books will be found in the above authorities.

Chapter I is, in the main, a summary of Sir H. H. Risley's views as expressed in Chapter VI of Vol. I of the *Imperial Gazetteer*. That is inevitable, since the *Gazetteer* contains necessarily the most authoritative summary of what is known on the subject, pending the appearance of Mr Gait's forthcoming Census Report.

Chapter II

The standard authority on the modern languages of India is Sir G. A. Grierson's work on *The Languages of India* (Calcutta, 1903). It will, however, be superseded by the book which Sir G. A. Grierson is now writing on the basis of the further materials collected in his *Linguistic Survey*, and in the Census Reports of 1911. The eleven volumes hitherto published of the *Survey* itself give specimens of the Indian languages and skeleton grammars.

Chapter III

Professor Macdonell's *History of Sanskrit Literature* (Heinemann, 1905) contains a fascinating and readable account of the Hindu scriptures from the Vedic ages up to modern times.

Professor Hopkins' *Religions of India* and *India Old and New* deal with both the literature and the actual working of Indian religions. Mr W. Crooke's *Native Races of Northern India* is a popular account of the Aryan region, and Mr Thurston's *Castes and Tribes of Southern India*. Madras, Government Press. 1908. Though it is more elaborate and scientific in its treatment, is full of matters which are interesting not only to the specialist.

Meredith Townsend's *Asia and Europe*. London. Archibald Constable. 1905. Is still an interesting and suggestive study of the differences between East and West, and Sir A. C. Lyall's *Asiatic Studies* are the even more illuminating results of a long, intimate, and sympathetic familiarity with Indian religious thought.

The chapter on Religion in the forthcoming Census Report for 1911 will contain the latest fruits of research, statistical and other.

There is an enormous mass of literature dealing in detail with the religions and sects of India. A selected list of books will be found at p. 446 of the *Imperial Gazetteer*.

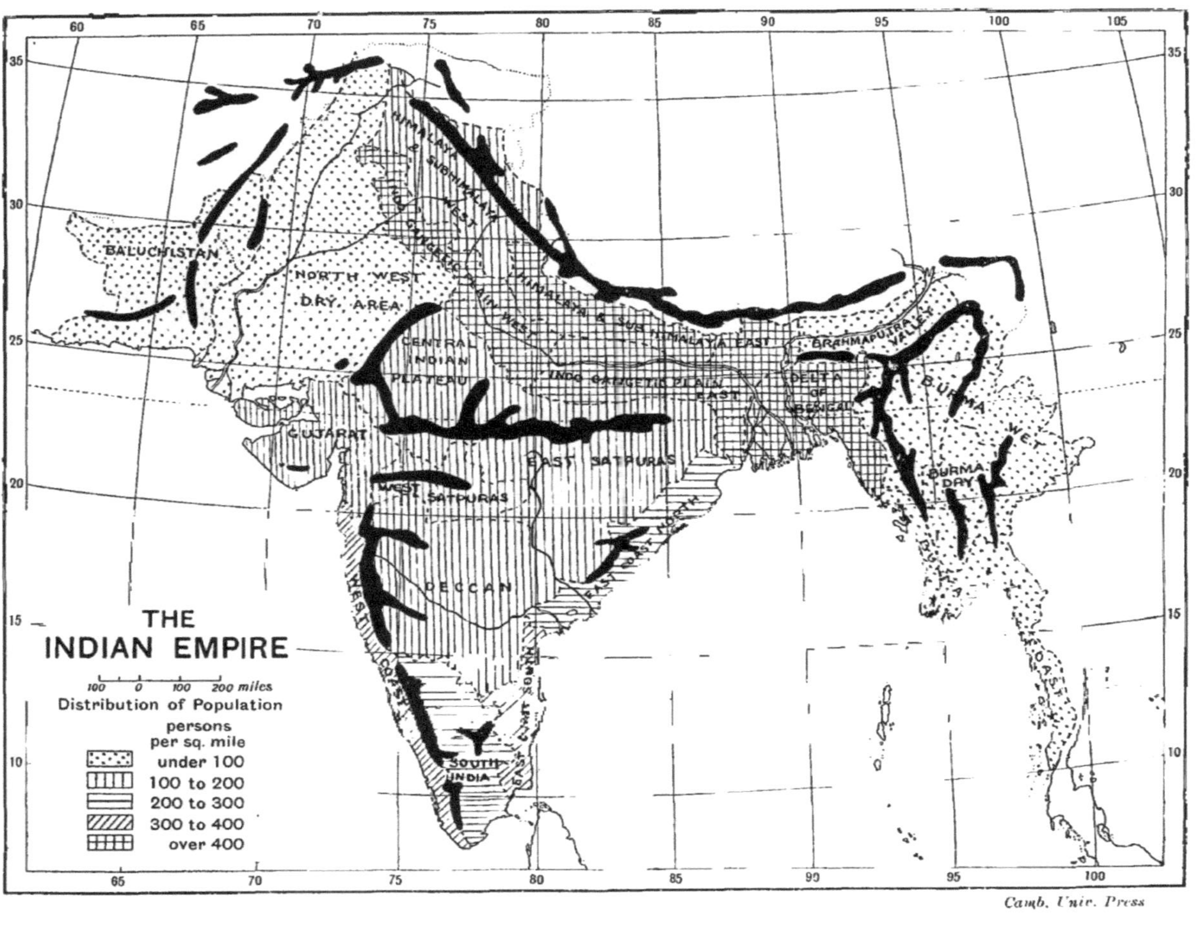

The Indian Empire—Distribution of Population

Camb. Univ. Press

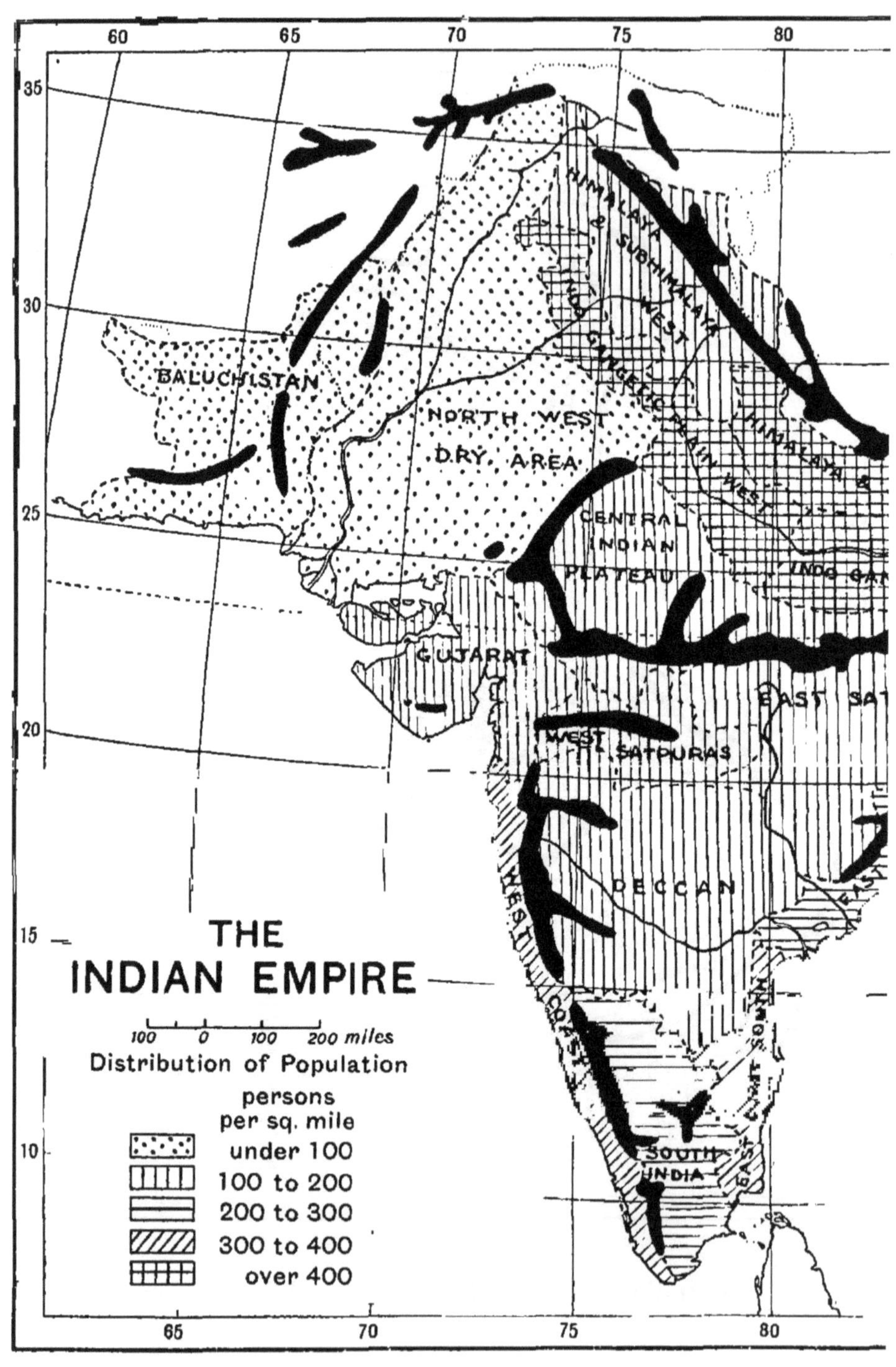

The Indian Empire—Distribution of Population (Enlarged - Left)

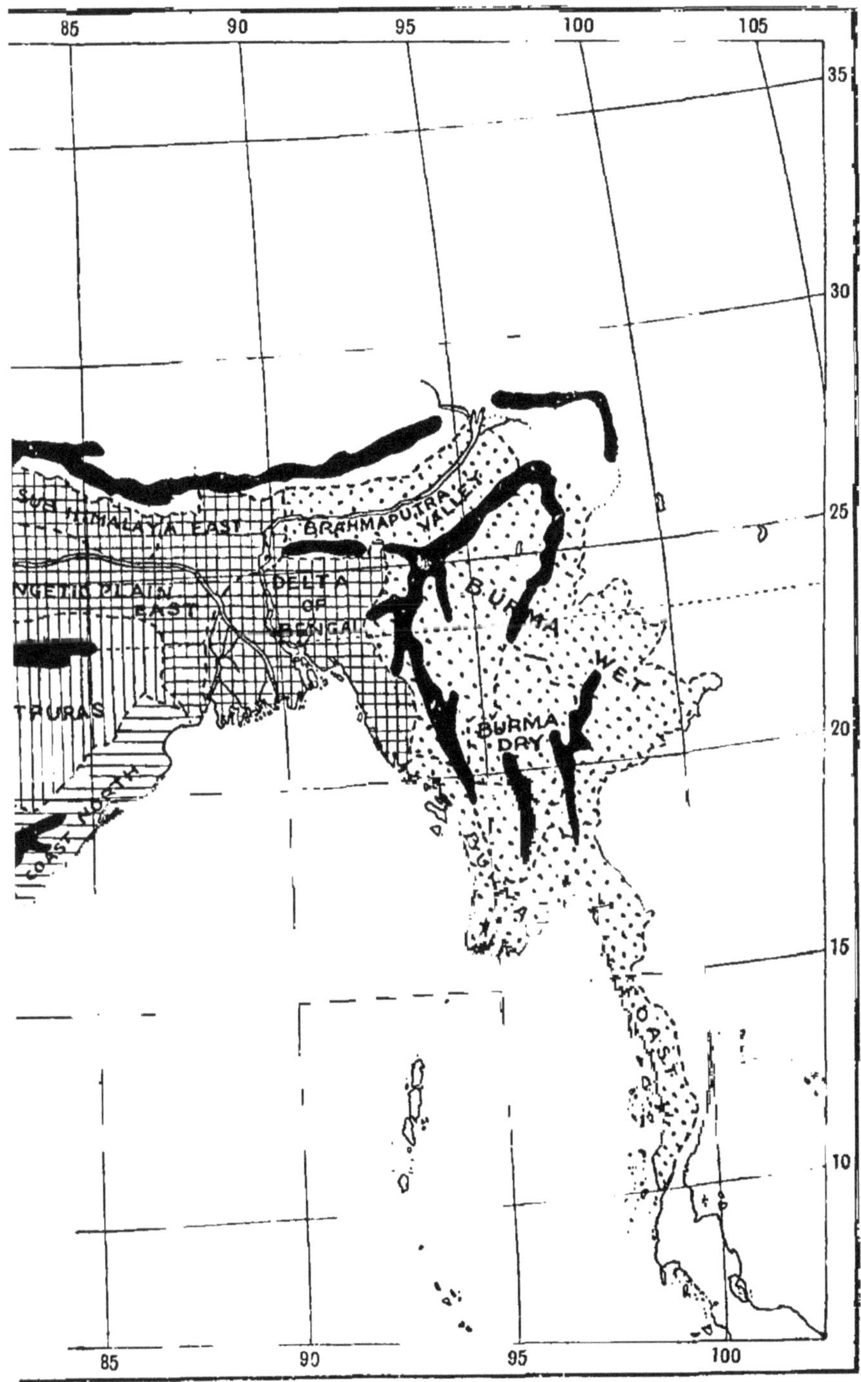

The Indian Empire—Distribution of Population (Enlarged - Right)

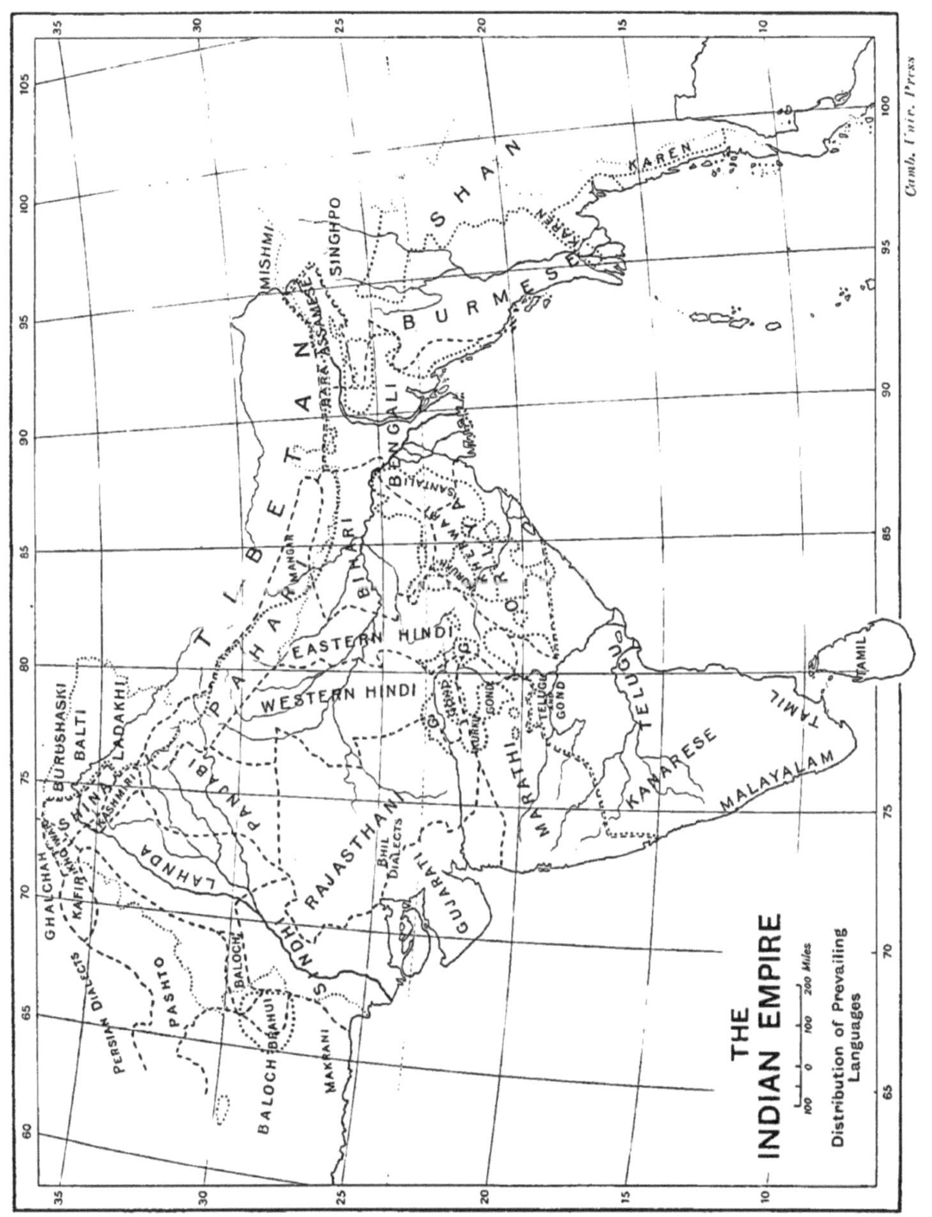

The Indian Empire—Distribution of Prevailing Languages

Camb. Univ. Press

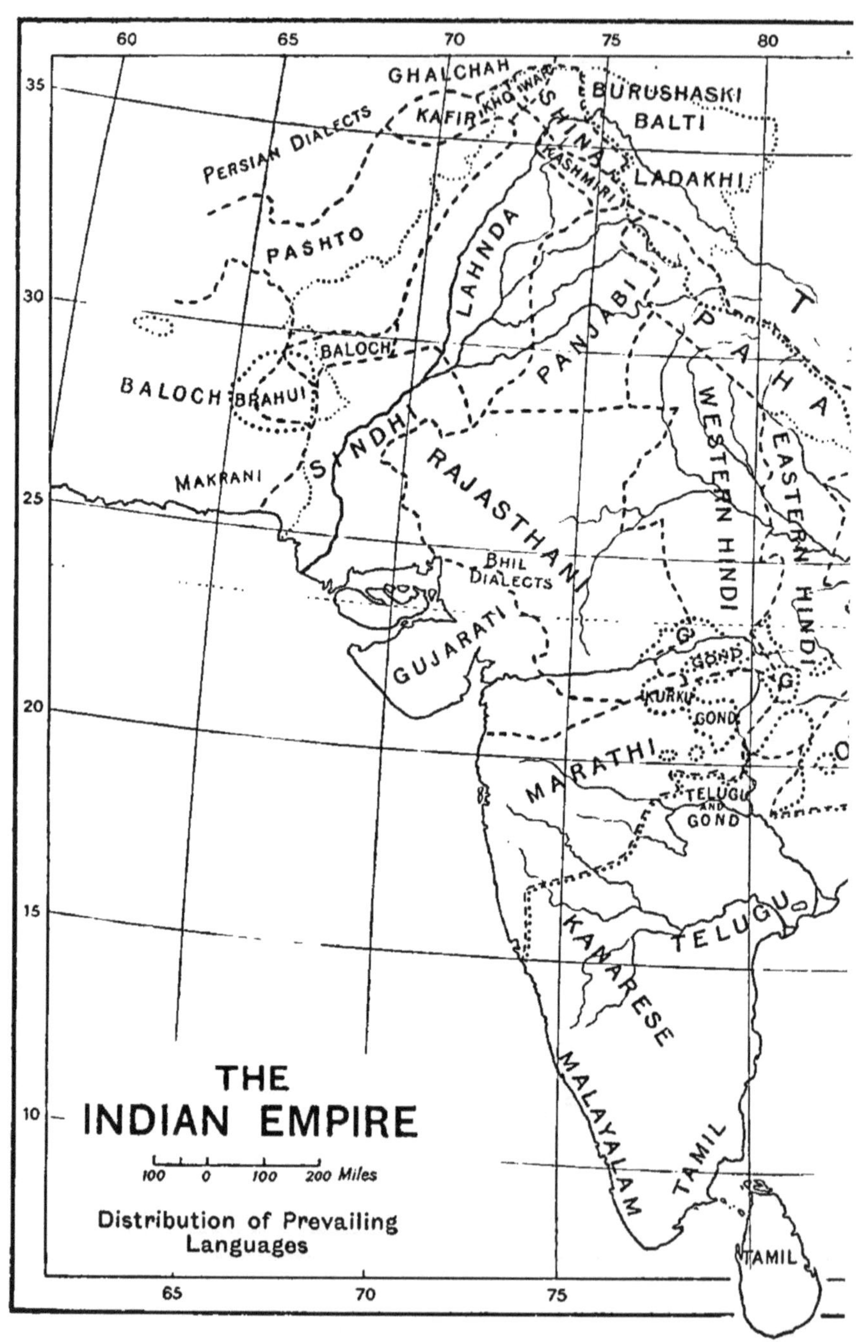

The Indian Empire—Distribution of Prevailing Languages (Enlarged - Left)

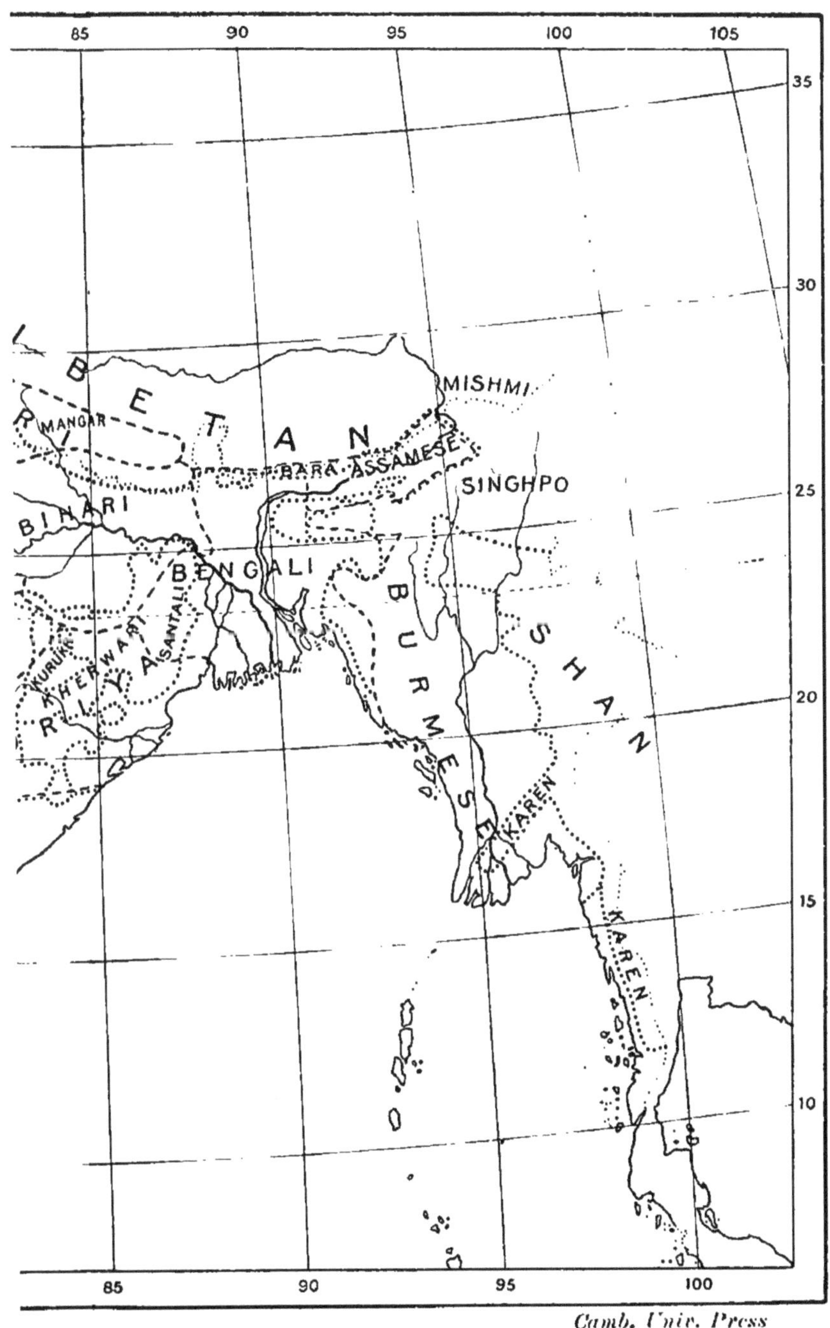

The Indian Empire—Distribution of Prevailing Languages (Enlarged - Right)

Index

C

D

F

G

H

I

J

K

L

M

N

O

P

R

S

W

Y

Printed by Libri Plureos GmbH in Hamburg,
Germany